## FIN KENNEDY

Fin Kennedy is an award-winning playwright of theatre and radio, whose plays are regularly produced in the UK and abroad. In 2021 he set up Applied Stories, a digital production company making audio drama and online training.

Fin's first play *Protection* was produced at Soho Theatre in 2003, where he was also Pearson writer-in-residence. His second play *How To Disappear Completely and Never Be Found* won the 38th Arts Council John Whiting Award and has been produced around the world. It has become a firm favourite with student and amateur performance groups and is among Nick Hern Books' most licensed plays.

Fin has twenty years' experience writing for teenagers, often through a process of being embedded in an inner-city school or youth theatre. Fin's first two plays for teenagers, *Locked In* (2006) and *We Are Shadows* (2008), were produced by Half Moon Young People's Theatre and toured nationally. *Life Raft* (2015), for Bristol Old Vic Young Company, has been translated into German and French for use in schools across Europe.

From 2006–2014 Fin was writer-in-residence at Mulberry School for Girls in East London, for whom he has written seven plays, published in two volumes by Nick Hern Books as *The Urban Girl's Guide to Camping and Other Plays* and *The Domino Effect and Other Plays for Teenagers*.

Fin also writes for radio and has had ten Afternoon Plays broadcast on BBC Radio 4 including *The Good Listener*, a returning series set inside GCHQ, and *On Kosovo Field*, a collaboration with musician PJ Harvey.

Fin's most recent venture is the UK's first fully online *Playwrighting for Teachers* course, to pass on many of the original creative-writing exercises he has devised over the years.

www.appliedstories.co.uk
www.playwrightingforteachers.co.uk

## Other Original Plays for Young People to Perform from Nick Hern Books

100 Christopher Heimann, Neil Monaghan, Diene Petterle

BANANA BOYS Evan Placey

BOYS Ella Hickson

BRAINSTORM Ned Glasier, Emily Lim and Company Three

BROKEN BISCUITS Tom Wells

BURYING YOUR BROTHER IN THE PAVEMENT Jack Thorne

THE CHANGING ROOM Chris Bush

CHAOS Laura Lomas

COCKROACH Sam Holcroft

COMMENT IS FREE James Fritz

THE DOMINO EFFECT AND OTHER PLAYS Fin Kennedy

THE FALL James Fritz

GIRLS LIKE THAT Evan Placey

IS MY MICROPHONE ON? Jordan Tannahill

THE IT Vivienne Franzmann

MOTH Declan Greene

PRONOUN Evan Placey

SAME Deborah Bruce

SHOUT Alexis Zegerman

THE SMALL HOURS Katherine Soper

START SWIMMING James Fritz

STUFF Tom Wells

THE TRIALS Dawn King

TUESDAY Alison Carr

THE URBAN GIRL'S GUIDE TO CAMPING AND OTHER PLAYS Fin Kennedy

THE WARDROBE Sam Holcroft

WHEN THEY GO LOW Natalie Mitchell

WHEN THIS IS OVER Ned Glasier, Sadeysa Greenaway-Bailey and Company Three

## Platform

Platform is a series of plays for young actors with all or mainly female casts, which put young women and their stories at the heart of the action – commissioned by Tonic Theatre, published and licensed by Nick Hern Books.

BRIGHT. YOUNG. THINGS. Georgia Christou

HEAVY WEATHER Lizzie Nunnery

THE GLOVE THIEF Beth Flintoff

THE LIGHT BURNS BLUE Silva Semerciyan

RED Somalia Seaton

SECOND PERSON NARRATIVE Jemma Kennedy

THIS CHANGES EVERYTHING Joel Horwood

For more information, visit www.tonictheatre-platform.co.uk

Fin Kennedy

# LIFE RAFT

*after Georg Kaiser's*
The Raft of the Medusa

*with interactive games
by Tassos Stevens
and Fin Kennedy*

NICK HERN BOOKS
London
www.nickhernbooks.co.uk

**A Nick Hern Book**

*Life Raft* first published in Great Britain in 2024 as a paperback original by Nick Hern Books Limited, The Glasshouse, 49a Goldhawk Road, London W12 8QP

*Life Raft* copyright © 2024 Fin Kennedy
*Life Raft: The Games* copyright © 2024 Tassos Stevens and Fin Kennedy

Fin Kennedy and Tassos Stevens have asserted their moral right to be identified as the authors of this work

Cover image: Extra Strong

Designed and typeset by Nick Hern Books, London
Printed in the UK by Mimeo Ltd, Huntingdon, Cambridgeshire PE29 6XX

A CIP catalogue record for this book is available from the British Library

ISBN 978 1 83904 404 5

**CAUTION**  All rights whatsoever in this play are strictly reserved. Requests to reproduce the text in whole or in part should be addressed to the publisher.

**Amateur Performing Rights**  Applications for performance, including readings and excerpts, by amateurs in the English language throughout the world should be addressed to the Performing Rights Department, Nick Hern Books, The Glasshouse, 49a Goldhawk Road, London W12 8QP, *tel* +44 (0)20 8749 4953, *email* rights@nickhernbooks.co.uk, except as follows:

*Australia*: ORiGiN Theatrical, Level 1, 213 Clarence Street, Sydney NSW 2000, *tel* +61 (2) 8514 5201, *email* enquiries@originmusic.com.au, *web* www.origintheatrical.com.au

*New Zealand*: Play Bureau, 20 Rua Street, Mangapapa, Gisborne, 4010, *tel* +64 21 258 3998, *email* info@playbureau.com

**Professional Performing Rights**  Applications for performance by professionals in any medium and in any language throughout the world should be addressed to Curtis Brown Ltd, Cunard House, 15 Regent Street, London, SW1Y 4LR, *tel* +44 (0)20 7393 4400, *fax* +44 (0)20 7393 4401, *email* cb@curtisbrown.co.uk

No performance of any kind may be given unless a licence has been obtained. Applications should be made before rehearsals begin. Publication of this play does not necessarily indicate its availability for amateur performance.

www.nickhernbooks.co.uk/environmental-policy

## Foreword

*Tom Morris*
*Artistic Director of Bristol Old Vic, 2009–2022*

It seems like a world away. The red-trousered philanthropist George Ferguson was elected as Bristol's first mayor in 2012, and his team put together a bid for the city to be Britain's first Green Capital. The roots of Bristol's Green revolution had been growing for decades, and in 2015 the year-long celebration was launched. Ferguson had asked Manchester Festival Director Alex Poots about the role of culture in city regeneration and as a result had insisted that Bristol's creative industries be drawn into the planning. Within the same week, Arcadia's Spider spouted green fire into the skies above Queen's Square, and Bristol Old Vic opened an ambitious play created for and with young people from across the region.

The project was the idea of the director Melly Still, and its text was a reimagination of Georg Kaiser's *The Raft of the Medusa*, here published for the first time as Fin Kennedy's *Life Raft*. Asking daring questions about the social consequences of climate change, the production resonated as a cry from the hearts of the young people onstage to the generation in power to avert climate catastrophe. It was a prophetic piece of theatre and its message is more urgent today than it has ever been.

*Melly Still*
*Director of Life Raft, 2015*

The original cast will be in their twenties now – and I can't help but wonder what memories they have of the summer we delved into this starkly prescient play. And what do I recall? A luminous group of young people joyously confident of commanding the main stage of the Bristol Old Vic. In fact, they began their story by clambering over the seats of the audience as if clinging on to ocean flotsam in a bid to reach their life raft. They were tirelessly playful and serious in their grasp of character; backstories were detailed and discussions around the themes were invigorating.

The life raft in the story is full of survivors between the ages of eight and thirteen, and having no other references, they act out their adult role models, initially adopting their belief systems as they try to work out how to survive. Sawn-off chairs and crates – angled to give the impression of bobbing hazardously in water – litter the stage and become symbols of an established hierarchy in the group. Those at the bottom are at the mercy of those at the top. Superstition versus reason dominates their discussions, and inevitably scapegoating and its accompanying rituals come into focus.

Looking back, it's striking that this production took place before social media and its unstable moral core began to orchestrate cultural camps, because the behaviour underpinning this is something the play investigates unflinchingly. And in a world that, ten years on, needs no reminding of what a life raft looks like, Fin Kennedy's incisive adaptation shifts from Georg Kaiser's *denkspiel* (a play about an idea or a mind game) and shines a light on the fears and hopes of the people on board. And being ten years older myself, I can't help but think of those people as our children and grandchildren…

## Introduction
*Fin Kennedy*

When director Melly Still first asked me to read Georg Kaiser's *The Raft of the Medusa*, I couldn't help but be struck by its bleakness.

It is a play about survival – and about human nature. But far from being about optimism, cooperation or triumph in adversity, it is about survival's dark side: madness, paranoia, and the desperate need for control. The play examines how, under the pressure-cooker circumstances of a life-and-death situation, these instincts can cause us to turn on one another with lethal consequences, and how even the most innocent of us – children – are not immune.

*The Raft of the Medusa* was German playwright Georg Kaiser's last play. Written in 1945, when he was in exile from Nazi Germany, it takes place on a lifeboat adrift in the Atlantic, filled with children after a passenger liner carrying British evacuees to Canada was torpedoed by German U-boats. Undiscovered for seven days, the thirteen children become obsessed with the idea that their number means they are cursed, and that only some kind of chilling sacrifice will save them. It was Kaiser's last play before he died, and reflects his despair at seeing the civilised world he thought he knew tear itself apart.

It was shocking to discover that these events were based on a true story. In September 1940, the steam-turbine ocean liner *SS City of Benares* left Liverpool for Canada. It was an evacuee ship carrying ninety children among 408 passengers and crew. Four days into its journey, in a remote part of the Atlantic, 630 miles from the nearest inhabited land, the *Benares* was spotted by a German U-boat and struck by two torpedoes. It sank in thirty-one minutes, with the loss of 260 lives, including seventy-seven of the evacuated children, aged five to thirteen years old. The sinking caused such outrage in Britain that it led to Winston Churchill cancelling the government's international evacuation programme in its entirety.

One of the *Benares*' lifeboats was indeed adrift for a week before being found, though the story that only children were on board appears to have been Kaiser's invention. In reality, there were only six boys aged eleven to thirteen, along with around forty adults, a mixture of chaperones, paying passengers and the ship's crew. They had food for three weeks but only one week's fresh water. They were eventually spotted by an RAF sea plane, and rescued by a naval destroyer. Individual survivors' stories proved impossible to find, but neither was there any evidence of things turning macabre on board in the way that Kaiser imagines.

But as a writer, he had found his allegory. The idea was a powerful device to anatomise the psychological weaknesses in all human beings, which had so recently destroyed Kaiser's own nation. In locating the action among children, war becomes an adult curse that the children do not understand, yet are doomed to repeat. The play is a searing indictment of the world of which these children are a product.

In creating the contemporary adaptation that became *Life Raft*, this historical material was a useful stimulus for a workshop week with Bristol Old Vic's Young Company. We deconstructed Kaiser's original text and built it back up again, adding more detail and personality to each of the characters than Kaiser had. (In his original, with the exception of Allan, Ann and Foxy, all the children simply have numbers rather than names.)

We also made two important further changes: The first was to elide Allan and Ann's culpability for the ending. In the original, Ann was the manipulative and malevolent force, with Allan the innocent, though impotent, saviour. In our version, it is the nexus between the two of them that is to blame. (We also swapped which of them experiences the great howl of regret at the end.)

The second big change was a steer from Bristol Old Vic's then artistic director, Tom Morris. Tom felt that the 1940's setting potentially let a modern audience dismiss it as a period piece – that the events in this context, though horrifying, could easily be written off as the baffling behaviour of a different age, when superstition was more powerful and people more easily led.

For Kaiser, there was nothing baffling about human beings turning on one another in the most brutal way. Indeed, he had in turn taken his title from an 1819 painting by French Romantic painter Théodore Géricault, depicting the aftermath of another real-world naval wreck, when the desperate crew resorted to cannibalism.

Any adaptation that is to remain true to Kaiser's original intent would need to implicate its contemporary viewers as powerfully as these two historical predecessors. And so it was that we alighted on a slightly timeless, though clearly modern, near-future dystopia, in which the children have grown up against a backdrop of a nameless war so long-lasting that none of them can remember anything else.

Melly Still's inspired original production for Bristol Old Vic's Young Company did not make for easy viewing, not least because all the roles were played by child actors of the same age. But nor was it without hope. There are moments of kindness and selflessness. The fundamental decency that is children's default mode, in the play becomes a bulwark against which the forces of hysteria must pit themselves for some time before they prevail. Perhaps with another roll of the dice, things would have turned out differently. Our children's innate grace remains our best hope.

I'm delighted that this published edition is accompanied by three new interactive games for groups, inspired by the world of the play and created by award-winning games designer Tassos Stevens:

*The Biscuit Game* takes the isolation of the lifeboat, with its limited supply of food, and unknowable rescue date, to introduce a playable scenario about the politics of survival.

*Angel Academy* introduces the role of storytellers to shape the events and tempo of a plot.

*A Life Well Played* provides a thoughtful framework for actors involved in an improvisation to assess afterwards how well they conveyed their characters' values, persona and relationships.

All three will not only enrich any young actor's experience of the play, they also serve as an introduction to game design for young performers, which is also of course an introduction to devising new stories. Intended for use either by young casts rehearsing the play, or as a stimulus for entirely new improvisations, the ingenious yet simple game mechanics created by Tassos Stevens and colleagues allow for an open world in which players must negotiate and make moral choices of their own.

Particular thanks are due to the three schools who helped us playtest these games during the summer of 2024: Whitmore School, Harrow, and teacher Signe Reinhold; Bishop Douglass School, Barnet, and teacher Erin Holland; and Mulberry School for Girls, and teachers Alison Hargreaves and Dawn Reid.

In this way, I hope we have opened up Georg Kaiser's powerful story as a contemporary arena in which infinite future possibilities can play out.

Some, I hope, will have happier endings.

*Life Raft* was first performed by the Young Company at Bristol Old Vic Theatre on 2 September 2015, with the following cast:

| | |
|---|---|
| MARGARET | Alyssa Thomas |
| MARGOT | Tilly Bennett |
| ANTHEA | Beth Carriaga |
| ENID | Courtnei-Violet Danks |
| SAM | Callum Harrison Deans |
| ARCHIE | Llewy Godfrey |
| ROGER | Jacob Bishop |
| FOXY | Charlie Cleaver |
| ALLAN | Toby Yapp |
| ALFIE | Oscar Adams |
| ANN | Amy Kemp |
| GEORGE | Kai Ball |
| AMY | Iris Supple-Still |
| ADULTS (*non-speaking*) | Fionn Gill |
| | Zara Ramm |
| *Director* | Melly Still |
| *Set and Costume Designer* | Max Johns |
| *Lighting Designer* | Tim Streader |
| *Sound and Composition* | Dave Price |
| *Costume Supervisor* | Pam Tait |
| *Production Manager* | David Miller |
| *Assistant Directors* | Miriam Battye |
| | James Kent |

## Characters

ALLAN, *fourteen, thinker, impressionable, reluctant leader*
ANN, *thirteen, cocky, confident, frightened*
GEORGE, *twelve, caring, jealous, easily led*
ALFIE, *thirteen, gruff, stubborn, physically strong*
ARCHIE, *twelve, gentle, kind, terrified*
ROGER, *thirteen, chivalrous, logical, sceptical*
SAM, *twelve, laddy, gullible, daydreamer*
MARGARET, *twelve, hysterical, competitive, afraid*
MARGOT, *eleven, immature, obedient, religious*
ENID, *thirteen, pugnacious, superior, judgemental*
ANTHEA, *eleven, kind, innocent, practical*
AMY, *eleven, introverted, traumatised, seriously injured*
FOXY, *nine, shell-shocked, silent, bright-red hair*

*Note: All these parts should be played by actors as close to the characters' ages as possible.*

## Setting

The action takes place over six days on board a lifeboat adrift at sea. It is inspired by a true story.

**A Note on Staging**

I would encourage any young company performing this play to find their own imaginative staging solutions to the effects called for in the script. For example, it may not be necessary to build a mock-up of a real lifeboat (and indeed to do so could restrict, rather than serve, the dramatic action – not to mention audience sightlines). Be bold, be theatrical. Impressionistic techniques are fine.

There is also the opportunity for each company to devise their own dream sequences between each scene. This is of course not compulsory, but remember that each scene is one day, so each interlude between scenes must be the night-time. In the original 2015 production at Bristol Old Vic, directed by Melly Still, we saw non-verbal dream sequences dreamt by four different characters and one 'shared' dream featuring everyone. These sections were highly stylised and increasingly nightmarish as the play goes on. I have not included descriptions of them in the script because I do not want to be prescriptive, and in any case I challenge you to find your own.

The only note I would give is that they should rely on imagery, sound, music and movement more than spoken text. They could also involve some additional non-speaking cast members who do not play one of the characters on board. These actors could be older, for example if one of the characters dreams about an older sibling, or their parents.

## Prologue

*Darkness.*

*The sound of the sea. Distantly, the sound of a war. The sound of the wind.*

*The sound of the sea. Darkness.*

## Day One

*A damp, grey dawn. Mist rises from a restless sea. A lifeboat fades into view. On its deck are huddled twelve children, in various positions of sleep: six boys and six girls aged between eleven and fourteen.*

*The eldest boy wears a white woollen scarf – this is* ALLAN.

*The eldest girl clutches a red Thermos flask tightly to her chest – this is* ANN. *The boat bobs gently as the sea sighs.*

ANN *is the first to wake. She sits up and looks around her slowly, fearfully – is this a dream? She surveys her sleeping companions. She looks out to the sea, and back again. Her lip wobbles, rising to a silent scream. She clutches herself tightly as she rocks back and forth. This cannot be real, this cannot be real…*

*She becomes aware of how tightly she is clutching the Thermos. She calms herself and loosens her grip. She unscrews the top, which is also a cup, fills it from the flask and drinks.*

ALLAN *awakes. He too surveys his surroundings slowly, with understated horror, until he notices* ANN. *Their eyes meet.*

ANN. What's the matter?

ALLAN. Nothing.

*Pause.*

ANN. Want some?

*ANN holds up the cup.*

ALLAN. Yes please.

*ANN pours.*

What is it?

ANN. Milk.

ALLAN. Oh.

ANN. Too big for a cup of milk?

ALLAN. I didn't say that.

*ANN finishes pouring and holds out the cup. ALLAN drinks.*

It's warm.

ANN. That's the idea.

ALLAN. When did you fill it?

ANN. Last night.

ALLAN. Before…

ANN. Yes, before.

*Pause.*

ALLAN. I wish I'd thought to save something.

ANN. You saved yourself.

ALLAN. So did you.

ANN. Were you scared?

ALLAN. No. Were you?

ANN. No.

*Pause. ANN scans the other sleeping children.*

I'd say we're the oldest here.

ALLAN. How old are you?

ANN. Thirteen. You?

ALLAN. Fourteen.

ANN. That makes you the leader.

*ALLAN takes off his scarf and hands it to her.*

What for?

ALLAN. It's what leaders do.

*ANN takes it.*

Thanks for the milk.

ANN. It isn't much.

ALLAN. It was kind. You're a leader too.

ANN. Let's share.

ALLAN. Can you have two leaders?

ANN. I mean the scarf.

ALLAN. Oh.

ANN. Half and half.

ALLAN. But I barely know you.

ANN. It doesn't mean we're engaged or anything.

*The scarf is quite long.* ANN *wraps one end round her neck and one round his. This inevitably brings them a bit closer.*

I'm Ann.

ALLAN. Allan.

*He offers his hand. She pecks him on the cheek instead. A moment.*

ANN. Allan and Ann.

ALLAN. Yes.

ANN. Two As. Must be top of the class.

*ALLAN smiles.* ANN *takes her end of the scarf off.*

Save it. You might need it.

ALLAN. Same.

*ALLAN hands back the empty milk cup.*

ANN. Every man for himself.

ALLAN. I'd say we're better off sticking together.

*The other children start to wake, the boys at first along one side of the boat:*

GEORGE, *followed by* ALFIE, *followed by* ARCHIE, *then* ROGER *and* SAM.

GEORGE. Where are we?

ALFIE. Where does it look like?

ARCHIE. All at sea. What t-time is it?

ROGER (*checking watch*). Six-thirty. On the dot.

SAM. I need a wee.

GEORGE. Where's our ship?

ARCHIE. G-gone.

ALFIE. Don't you remember?

SAM. Boom!

ROGER. I can still taste the smoke.

ARCHIE. M-me too.

ROGER. Yuck.

SAM. I almost died.

ALFIE. We all did.

ALLAN. Well we didn't. Be thankful.

ALFIE. Who are you?

ALLAN. I'm Allan. This is Ann.

ANN. This is our ship now.

ALFIE. Your ship?

ALLAN. All of us.

DAY ONE    19

ROGER. Until we're rescued.

ALFIE. When will that be?

ROGER. Soon.

SAM. How do you know?

ROGER. Because who'd leave us here?

SAM. Boom!

GEORGE. Stop it.

SAM. Boom!

GEORGE. Where's my sister? I need to find my sister. Evie? Evie!

ALFIE. Probably dead.

GEORGE. Shut up!

ARCHIE. D-don't say that!

ROGER. It's possible though.

ARCHIE. You d-don't know that.

GEORGE. She was – she was –

ALLAN. In the water?

GEORGE. Yes.

SAM. She might be on another boat then.

ARCHIE. We're only ch-children.

ALFIE. Speak for yourself.

ARCHIE. They wouldn't l-leave us.

ALFIE. I'm a man.

ROGER. How old are you?

ALFIE. Thirteen.

SAM. I'm only twelve.

ARCHIE. So am I.

GEORGE. So am I.

ALFIE. Babies.

ARCHIE. Sh-shut up.

GEORGE. Yeah you can't bully us.

ALFIE. Why not?

GEORGE. I'm taller than you.

ALFIE. So?

ROGER. I'm thirteen.

ANN. Well Allan's fourteen. He's the oldest.

SAM. You won't be rescued then. They'll only rescue children.

ALLAN. We'll all be rescued.

ANN. Yes, whenever children go missing it's taken seriously.

ALFIE. We're not all children.

ANN. We are to them.

GEORGE. Who?

ANN. Adults.

ALLAN. That's right. When something like this happens, it's on the news.

GEORGE. Ours was a whole ship of children.

ROGER. Then we'll be on the news right now.

SAM. Where's the cameras?

ROGER. Not like that. It'll be on the news that we're missing.

ALLAN. And that they're looking.

ROGER. That's right.

ALFIE. Well they'd better hurry. It's freezing.

GEORGE. Why were we attacked?

SAM. Boom!

ROGER. They'll already be out looking.

ARCHIE. Yeah, we'll be rescued any s-second.

ALFIE. What's wrong with your voice?

ARCHIE. N-nothing.

GEORGE. Well I can't see anyone coming.

SAM. Boom!

ROGER. Stop that.

GEORGE. Why would they attack children?

ALLAN. That's war.

ALFIE. That's right, just how it is.

ANN. It's because it hurts the adults.

GEORGE. But we haven't done anything.

ANN. Exactly.

ARCHIE. M-maybe it was an accident.

SAM. It was a bomb. From a plane.

ALFIE. It was a mine. In the sea.

ROGER. Could've been a torpedo. From a sub.

ANN. Does it matter?

ALLAN. We don't know what it was.

GEORGE. I was asleep.

ALLAN. We all were.

SAM. The explosion woke me up.

ALFIE. I saw the water coming in.

ARCHIE. I heard s-screaming.

ROGER. My cabin caught fire –

GEORGE. There was smoke –

ANN. Enough!

*Pause.*

ALLAN. Ann's right. We're safe now. Be thankful.

ALFIE. Thankful for what?

ALLAN. You're still alive, aren't you?

ALFIE. Well that depends.

ALLAN. They'll be here soon.

SAM. I thought maybe it was all a dream.

*Pause. Then, of the other sleeping children opposite:*

GEORGE. Who are they?

ROGER. Those are girls.

ALFIE. Yuck.

ANN. Er, excuse me.

ALLAN. We have to look after them.

SAM (*of* ANN). She's a girl.

ALLAN. She's got me.

*The girls begin to wake.*

MARGARET *first, then* MARGOT, *then* ENID, *then* ANTHEA, *and finally* AMY, *who is visibly injured.*

MARGARET. Oh my God, we're outdoors.

MARGOT (*crossing herself*). Hail Mary, full of grace, the Lord is with thee.

MARGOT *has a dolly, she crosses her dolly's heart too.*

ENID. Fffffreezing!

ROGER. I'll keep you warm.

ENID. Who are you?

ROGER. My name's Roger.

ENID. Get off.

ANTHEA. Where are we?

ALLAN. You're on a lifeboat, you're safe.

MARGARET (*of* AMY). Oh my God, look at her.

ENID. Oh my God.

ANTHEA. Oh my God.

MARGOT. Blood...

ARCHIE. B-blood!

MARGARET. Eurgh, blood.

MARGOT. Eurgh!

ALFIE. Is she dead?

ANN. Of course not, she's awake.

ALLAN. Well don't just sit there.

ANN. What should we do?

ALLAN. I don't know.

ANN. You're the oldest.

ALLAN. So?

MARGARET. Is he?

ANN. Yes, he's the leader.

MARGOT. Oh good.

ENID. Why does that make him the leader?

ALLAN. I'm not a doctor.

ENID. The best person should be leader not just the oldest.

ANTHEA. It's alright, my mum's a nurse.

MARGARET. Oh brilliant.

ENID. Help her then.

SAM. Yeah make her better.

GEORGE. How?

ANTHEA. You have to start by asking their name. (*To* AMY.) What's your name?

GEORGE. Doesn't she know her name?

ENID. Why can't a girl be the leader?

ANN. I'm second-in-command.

ENID. I'm third.

ANN. That's how it works on boats.

ROGER. It's called a mate.

ANN. I'm not your mate.

ROGER. That's what it's called.

ENID. I'm third-in-command.

ANN. Alright then.

ALFIE. Who's fourth?

ANN. There is no fourth.

ENID. That would be too many.

ANTHEA (*to* AMY). Can you speak? Say your name.

> AMY *tries to say her name but struggles to get it out.*
> ANTHEA *inspects* AMY*'s wounds, she gets blood on her.*

MARGARET. Oh my God, it's on your hands.

ANTHEA. Bandages, we need bandages.

ENID. There aren't any.

ANTHEA. There must be. It's a lifeboat.

SAM. She's a nurse.

ANTHEA. My mum is.

MARGOT. You must know everything.

ANTHEA. A bit. I know you need bandages to stop bleeding. Tied tight.

ROGER. Here. Use my shirt.

ALLAN. Really?

ANN. How?

ROGER. I'll tear it.

ALFIE. You'll freeze.

ROGER. It's already freezing.

MARGARET. We won't look.

ANN. It's fine for boys.

ROGER. She needs it more than me.

ALLAN. Good lad.

ENID. Yes, that's good of you.

GEORGE. Good lad.

ANTHEA. Thanks.

GEORGE. She can have my jumper too.

ALLAN. Yes, well done.

ANN. Well done.

ENID. Good boy.

ALLAN. That's how we'll get through this – together.

ANN. That's right.

ALLAN. Looking out for each other.

ROGER. Survivors.

ALLAN. Yes, survivors.

ANN. Survivors!

ALL. Survivors!

>ROGER *tears his shirt and* ANTHEA *uses the strips to wrap* AMY*'s wounds.*

ANN. I've got milk.

>ANN *holds up her flask.*

>It's still warm. Let's share.

ENID. Ooh yes.

MARGARET. Thank you.

MARGOT. That's kind.

ALFIE. Yeah go on then.

ARCHIE. Will there b-be enough?

ROGER. Ladies first

ANTHEA. Injured first.

ANN. That's right.

ALFIE. She's also a lady.

SAM. Can I wee in it after?

ROGER. Wee in what?

SAM. The flask.

ALL GIRLS. Eurgh!

MARGARET. No!

ANTHEA. Yuck!

ANN. Of course not.

ENID. Of course not.

MARGOT. You're horrid.

SAM. I'm desperate.

ALFIE. Go over the side.

SAM. What, in front of everyone?

ENID (*to* SAM). You need to learn some manners.

SAM. It's natural.

MARGOT. Not going in a flask.

SAM. I was only joking.

ENID. Well it didn't seem like it.

ANN. Hands up who wants some then. (*To* SAM.) Not you.

SAM. Oh, please.

*They all put their hands up except* ALLAN.

ALLAN. I've had some.

ANN. How many are we?

ALLAN. Twelve. But we've had some.

ENID (*of* SAM). And he's not getting any.

SAM. Oh don't be like that.

ARCHIE. There won't b-be enough. I won't have any.

SAM. Can I have yours?

ARCHIE. No.

ANN. There's enough. Allan and I had ours earlier. So that's ten.

ENID (*i.e. not* SAM). Well, nine.

SAM. That isn't fair!

ALLAN. Oh let him have some. You're sorry, aren't you?

SAM. I said so, didn't I?

ENID. And there'll be no weeing.

SAM. Promise.

ANN. Good. Now line up and let's do this properly.

*They stand up and form two lines. The boat wobbles a little.*

ARCHIE. C-careful of the boat!

ALFIE. It's fine.

ALLAN (*of* AMY). How is she?

ANTHEA. It looks like shrapnel.

MARGARET. Eurgh.

ANTHEA. Four pieces I think. And burns.

MARGOT. Poor thing.

ANN. She must go first. There's only one cup so I'll pour one at a time.

ALLAN. What's her name?

ANTHEA. I think she said Amy.

AMY *nods.*

ANN. Okay, listen. When it's your turn you have to say your name before drinking.

ENID. Good idea.

ANN. That way we'll get to know each other.

GEORGE. I'll write them down so we don't forget. I've got a pen and paper.

SAM. Let's see.

ANN. Here – for Amy.

*The first cup of milk is passed to* AMY. ANTHEA *helps her drink it.* AMY *struggles to say her name*

AMY (*weakly*). Amy.

GEORGE *writes it down.*

ANTHEA. Ssh, it's okay. You don't have to.

AMY. I want to.

ANTHEA. You're ill.

AMY. I'll be okay.

MARGARET. Oh God. Is she going to be okay?

ALLAN. Yes. We all are. We have to stay strong. Look after each other. Got that?

ALL. Yes.

ANN. Who's next?

ROGER. Ladies first.

ALLAN. Yes that's right.

ALFIE. That's how it should be.

ARCHIE. R-really?

GEORGE. Yes.

SAM. Oh alright then.

ALFIE. Shut up, you're not getting any.

MARGARET. Don't say 'shut up', it's rude.

ALFIE. Shut up.

MARGARET. You shut up.

ALFIE. *You* shut up.

MARGARET. Shut up.

ANN. Shut up, both of you.

ALFIE. Especially her.

MARGARET. Shut up!

ALLAN. Everyone shut up! (*Pause.*) Alright?

ANN. Thank you, Allan.

ALFIE. Who made him leader?

ANN. I did.

ALFIE. When?

ANN. Earlier.

GEORGE. I won't write down all those 'shut ups'.

MARGARET. Good.

GEORGE. It's a waste of paper.

ANN *pours and hands the second cup to* MARGARET.

ANN. Name.

MARGARET. Margaret. Not Maggie.

*Everyone murmurs 'Hello, Margaret, nice to meet you', etc.*

GEORGE. Margaret takes longer to write.

MARGARET. That's because it's proper.

MARGARET *drinks and hands the cup back.* ANN *pours a third and hands it to* MARGOT.

MARGOT. I'm Margot. Not Marge. And this is Lilly. (*Her dolly.*) Not Lil.

MARGOT *drinks and hands the cup back. Everyone murmurs 'Hello, Margot, hello, Lilly', etc.*

GEORGE. They're hard to spell.

MARGOT. Not if you know how.

GEORGE. Do I have to write down dollies too?

MARGOT. Yes.

ANN. No.

ALFIE. She's not real.

GEORGE. I'm not writing down not-real people.

ROGER. I agree with that.

MARGOT. I don't.

ENID. I do.

ANN. I do.

ALLAN. Yes, that settles it. Only real people go in the book. Sorry, Margot.

MARGOT. Don't apologise to me.

*MARGOT holds up her dolly Lilly.*

ALLAN. She's not real.

ENID. Not-real people don't get apologies.

GEORGE. Or names.

ANN. Or milk.

*ANN pours a fourth cup and hands it to ENID. ENID drinks first then says her name.*

ENID. Enid.

GEORGE. Nice and short.

*Everyone murmurs 'Hello, Enid', etc. ENID drinks and hands the cup back.*

ENID. Mmm, lovely and warm. Thank you.

ANN. You're welcome.

*ANN pours a fifth and hands it to ANTHEA.*

ANTHEA. Anthea.

*Everyone murmurs 'Hello, Anthea', etc.*

GEORGE. An-the-a?

ANTHEA. Yes.

GEORGE. Bloody hell.

ENID. If you can't write don't write.

MARGARET. You swore.

GEORGE. I can write.

MARGARET. Bloody's swearing.

GEORGE. So?

SAM. So? Who's to stop us?

ALFIE. Yeah we can do what we like.

ALLAN. I'm in charge.

ENID. Are you?

ALLAN. So is Ann.

ALFIE. And me.

ENID. And me.

ALLAN. No you're not.

ANN. You can't have more than two.

ALFIE. Who says?

ALLAN. We say.

ENID. I thought it was three?

ALLAN. Three's too many.

ANN (*of the milk*). Now the boys.

*ANN pours another cup and hands it to* GEORGE.

GEORGE. George.

ENID. Who's going to write your name?

GEORGE. I am.

*GEORGE drinks, hands the cup back, and writes.* ANN *pours another cup and hands it to* ALFIE.

ALFIE. Alfie Smart. Cheers.

*ALFIE downs it in one.*

ENID. Oh we didn't say surnames!

GEORGE. I'm not writing surnames too.

ANN. That's alright.

ENID. Mine's Clancy.

ALFIE. Oi – I've got the cup.

ENID. Sorry.

> ALFIE *hands the cup back.* ANN *pours another cup and hands it to* ARCHIE.

ARCHIE. I-is there enough?

ANN. Just about, I think.

ARCHIE (*indicates* ROGER *and* SAM, *who haven't had any yet*). What about these t-two?

ROGER. The girls have all had some. We don't matter so much. I can go for ages without eating.

SAM. I can't.

> ARCHIE *drinks.*

ENID. You have to say your name!

> ARCHIE *chokes.*

ALFIE. Slap him on the back.

ARCHIE. S-sorry.

ENID. Name!

ARCHIE. Ar-archie.

GEORGE (*writing*). 'Ar-archie'

ROGER. No it's not written like that.

GEORGE. That's how he said it.

ALFIE. He's disabled.

ARCHIE. No I'm n-not!

ROGER. No he's not.

ARCHIE. It's a s-stutter!

GEORGE. Well that's confusing.

ARCHIE. N-no it's not.

GEORGE. It's a waste of letters.

> ARCHIE *hands the cup back.* ANN *pours a ninth cup and hands it to* ROGER.

ROGER. Roger Hargreaves, at your service.

> ROGER *raises the cup like a toast, does a little bow, then drinks. The girls coo, the boys mutter.*

> ROGER *hands the cup back.* ANN *pours the tenth and final cup.*

ANN (*to* SAM). Now then.

ENID. Not him.

SAM. But Allan said I could.

MARGARET. You were naughty.

ALLAN. Let him have it.

MARGOT. Not just naughty – disgusting.

ANN. We can control that. Do you promise to behave?

SAM. Yes.

ENID. Do you promise not to be disgusting?

SAM. Yes.

ENID. Louder.

SAM. Yes I promise!

MARGOT. You tell him.

ANN. Then you can have some.

> ANN *hands the cup to* SAM.

ENID. What do you say?

SAM. Why do I get the last one?

ENID. Ungrateful!

MARGOT. Because you were disgusting!

ANN. Do you want it or not?

SAM. Yeah.

ENID. Then say thank you.

ALFIE. I'll have his.

SAM. Get off.

SAM *drinks quickly, before* ALFIE *can get any. He hands the cup back.*

Thanks.

MARGOT. That's better.

ENID. Name?

SAM. Sam.

ALL. Hello, Sam.

GEORGE. Another short one.

ENID. Short enough to forget.

GEORGE. No you won't. (*Waves his pad.*)

ANN. Now then. Twelve of us have had some and there's still some left.

ALLAN *has been sitting above them on the prow. He stands.*

ALLAN. We'll save the rest for whoever gets weak first.

ANTHEA. Amy's weak.

ALLAN. For Amy then.

MARGARET. Why would anyone else get weak?

SAM. If there's another bomb.

ALLAN. If it's a long time.

MARGOT. If what's a long time?

ALFIE. Before we get to shore.

ROGER. How will we get to shore? We're drifting.

ENID. How far is it?

ARCHIE. A l-long way.

ANTHEA. How do you know?

ARCHIE. I saw a m-map before we set off. The sea was m-massive.

ROGER. Hang on, we can work this out. Our ship set sail three days ago. (*Checking watch.*) At half past eight on the morning of the eleventh. It's now quarter to seven on the fourteenth. If we were sailing at an average of forty knots… who's good at maths?

MARGARET. Me!

ENID. Me!

ARCHIE. M-me!

ALFIE (*to* ROGER). Nice watch. Can I see?

ROGER. It's my dad's. He bought a new one so gave me his old one. It's Swiss. They're the best.

ALLAN. Why's that?

ROGER. Accuracy. They never lose a second, even if a million years goes by.

GEORGE. What's the answer then? To how far away we are.

ARCHIE. That's a hard s-sum.

MARGARET. It's quite far.

ENID. The answer is: Quite Far.

SAM. Look around. There's no land anywhere.

*Pause while they look around.*

ARCHIE. Nothing but s-sea.

GEORGE. And sky.

ALFIE. Quiet.

SAM. You wouldn't even know there's a war.

*MARGARET suddenly bursts into tears.*

ALFIE. Oh God.

ENID. There there.

ALFIE. Yeah make her stop.

MARGARET *continues to cry.*

MARGARET. Why is there a war?

ALLAN. There's always been a war.

ANN. That's right.

ALLAN. Ever since I can remember.

ALFIE. And me.

ALLAN. It's about who owns things.

MARGARET (*sobbing*). What things?

ANTHEA. Everything.

SAM. Land.

ARCHIE. F-food.

ROGER. Other people.

ENID. That's how things get decided.

ANN. Sometimes there isn't a reason. Everyone just decides they hate each other.

ALFIE. And that some people should die.

ALLAN. Those are the worst ones, because then they never end.

MARGARET. Is this one one of those ones?

GEORGE. Probably.

ALFIE. Definitely.

SAM. I reckon.

ROGER. Well it definitely isn't ending.

MARGARET. Well kids would never do a war to each other, not ever!

ALFIE. But the adults do.

MARGARET. And now we're stuck!

GEORGE. Stuck here and we might never be rescued.

MARGARET *wails. The other girls comfort her.*

ROGER. Of course we'll be rescued.

MARGARET. When?

ALLAN. Soon.

MARGARET. When?

ROGER. Tomorrow.

ALLAN. That's right.

SAM. How do they know?

GEORGE. Roger's got a watch. It's Swiss.

MARGARET. I'm scared.

MARGOT. Ssh, it's alright.

MARGARET. I want my dad.

SAM. Make her stop.

ALFIE. Yeah, I can't stand crying women.

ARCHIE *starts crying.*

ARCHIE. I'm scared t-too.

ENID. Oh for goodness' sake.

ARCHIE. Are we g-going to die?

ALLAN. No!

ARCHIE. How d-do you know?

ALFIE. Oh shut up, you girl.

MARGARET / MARGOT / ENID / ANTHEA. Oi.

ALLAN. No one's doing any dying.

MARGOT. Amy might.

ANTHEA. Don't say that!

AMY. I don't want to die.

ANTHEA. You won't.

ALFIE. No one *wants* to die.

ALLAN. And they won't.

ANN. Yes, we've got milk.

ALLAN. We've got each other.

ANN. That's right. We mustn't talk about how scared we are. Even a little bit.

ALLAN. Ann's right. It's bad for morale.

ENID. Look – I've got a magic piece of chalk. If you draw a circle around something it protects it.

ARCHIE. R-really?

ENID. I'll draw a circle round the boat.

ANTHEA. That's brilliant. Isn't that brilliant?

ENID *draws a circle all round the edge of the boat.*

ARCHIE. Does it mean we'll b-be rescued?

ANTHEA. Definitely.

ALLAN. Probably.

ROGER. They're probably already on their way.

ARCHIE. C-careful of rocking it!

ENID. It's worth it if it protects us.

MARGARET (*to* ARCHIE). Pull yourself together!

ARCHIE. I'm s-sorry.

ALLAN. We need to do a search.

ALL. Yeah!

ALLAN. Every nook and cranny. There's bound to be some supplies.

ROGER. Or a radio.

ALFIE. Or a flare.

ALLAN. In every lifeboat they store things for a grown-up crew, things to last them ages, for exactly this situation.

GEORGE. Let's go!

ROGER. Boys do the left, girls do the right.

ALFIE. It's port and starboard on a boat.

ROGER. What is?

ALFIE. Left and right.

ROGER. Just so long as we do them both.

SAM. And front and back.

ALFIE. That's got special words too.

ROGER. What are they?

ALFIE. I can't remember.

ANN. Stop yapping, start searching.

*They all search the boat. They find four large oars.*

SAM. Look – flippers!

ALFIE. They're called oars, dumbo.

SAM. Shut up, I'm not dumb.

ENID. Help me, they're heavy.

ANTHEA. Mind Amy!

ENID. Well she is taking up lots of space.

ANTHEA. She's ill.

ENID. I know.

ANTHEA. She needs to lie down.

ALFIE. Does she have to lie across the middle like that?

*ANTHEA tries to move AMY, who groans.*

ANTHEA (*to* AMY). I'm sorry, you're in the way. (*To others.*) Help me then.

*Some others help ANTHEA move AMY. Everyone else is grappling with oars.*

ALLAN. Three to an oar!

ANN. Stick them in those holes!

ROGER. They'll fall in the water!

ANN. No they won't, that's where they go!

ALLAN. Rowlocks!

ALFIE. What?

ALLAN. That's the name for them, the holes.

ANN. Allan's right. I've rowed before so I know.

ALLAN. Where have you rowed?

ANN. My uncle's lake.

ALLAN. Your uncle has a lake?

ANN. He did. Before.

*They set all four oars.*

ALFIE. 'Rowlocks.'

ROGER. Rows locked!

ENID. Still, we can't eat oars, can we?

MARGOT. Yes, I'm hungry.

*A chorus of: 'So am I', 'And me', 'Me too', etc.*

ALLAN. Hang on, there's something else.

*He pulls out a sail.*

MARGARET. Is it a blanket?

ALLAN. It's a sail.

MARGARET. If it's a blanket bagsy I have it.

MARGOT. We can all have it.

ALLAN. Hang on, there's more.

ALLAN *takes out a bucket for bailing water. He hands it to* SAM.

Take this.

SAM. What for?

ALLAN. What do you think?

SAM. Weeing?

ENID. Eurgh.

ALFIE. And the rest.

MARGOT. Don't.

ALLAN. It's for bailing water.

MARGOT. Why would we need to do that?

ROGER. If we start sinking.

MARGOT. Oh!

ALLAN. We won't sink.

SAM. We might if we all hold in our wee.

*ALLAN hands SAM the bucket.*

ALLAN. Make a curtain with the sail.

SAM. Why me?

ALLAN. Because you need to go.

SAM. I don't mind being seen.

ENID. Filthy!

ALLAN. Well the ladies mind seeing you.

SAM. But –

ALLAN. Do it.

*SAM sulkily sets up a toilet area at one end of the boat, with the bucket behind the sail.*

ANN. Is there more?

ALLAN. Looks like it.

*With some effort,* ALLAN *pulls out a large drawstring canvas bag filled with tins.*

Tins!

ALL. Yay!

ANN. What sort?

ALLAN. Biscuits, tinned ham –

ALFIE. Supplies!

ALLAN. And water!

ALL. Hooray!

MARGOT. Thank the Lord!

ENID. Thank the lifeboat.

ROGER. We're saved!

ENID. Oh but wait I'm vegetarian.

MARGOT. I'm starving!

ANTHEA. Me too!

SAM. Give it here!

ENID. I'll need more biscuits!

GEORGE. Get off, you'll drop them!

ALLAN. Wait –

*They grab the canvas bag from* ALLAN *and tear it open. Tins scatter everywhere. The boat wobbles as they lunge for them.*

Careful!

ARCHIE. Mind the b-boat!

ALLAN. One at a time!

ANN. You'll drop them overboard!

GEORGE. This will last ages – we're smaller than adults.

ALLAN. Stop running!

ROGER. Let the girls get them, they should go first.

SAM. Biscuits for breakfast!

ALL. Yay!!

ANN (*authoritatively*). Wait!

*They all stop.*

DAY ONE    43

These are tins. There must be a tin opener.

ALLAN *searches in the bottom of the drawstring bag. Everyone holds their breath.*

There must be.

ALLAN *pulls one out and holds it aloft. They all breathe a sigh of relief.*

ALL. Hooray!

MARGOT. We can eat!

MARGARET. We're saved!

ANN *snatches the tin opener from* ALLAN.

ANN. This – is the most precious item on this entire boat. More precious than any of us. It must be kept safe. I'll look after it.

ANN *pockets the tin opener.* MARGOT *hands* ANN *a tin.*

MARGOT. Please can you open this one?

ANN *opens it. It takes a moment – there is some anticipation.*

ENID. What's inside?

MARGOT. The label's faded.

MARGARET. Why did you pick that one?

MARGOT. It rattled.

ALFIE. Is it ham?

MARGOT. No, it rattled.

ROGER. Is it sweets?

ARCHIE. It – it might be.

GEORGE. It might be jelly beans.

SAM. I hope it's custard.

ANTHEA. Me too.

MARGOT. Custard doesn't rattle, stupid.

SAM. Piss off, I'm not stupid.

MARGARET. You swore.

SAM. So?

MARGARET. You're not getting anything.

SAM. You're not in charge – (*Of* ANN.) she is.

ANN *opens it. She looks inside.*

ANN. Biscuits.

ALL. Yay!

GEORGE. What kind?

ENID. Beggars can't be choosers.

GEORGE. I'm not a beggar.

ROGER. Yes, speak for yourself.

ANN. Digestives.

GEORGE. Chocolate?

ANN. No.

GEORGE. Boring.

ALLAN. I'll have some.

ALFIE. And me.

ENID. And me.

ALLAN. Littlest first.

ANTHEA. Injured first.

ENID. Littlest first.

ANTHEA. Amy first.

ARCHIE. I-I'm littlest.

MARGOT. I am.

SAM. I am.

ALFIE. I'm not.

ENID (*to* ANTHEA, *of* AMY). She's too ill to eat, isn't she?

ANN. No, Anthea's right. Amy first.

ANTHEA (*to* AMY). Are you hungry? Do you think you can eat something?

AMY. I think so.

ANN. One biscuit each. No more, no less.

ENID. Smallest here, biggest there.

*ANN hands a biscuit to ANTHEA to give to AMY.*

AMY. Thank you, Ann.

*Everyone lines up to get a biscuit from ANN. ALLAN is still busy under the prow.*

ROGER. Can I borrow your pad?

GEORGE. Why?

ROGER. We need to work out rations.

GEORGE. What for?

ROGER. To make the best use of the food. I'll show you.

*GEORGE hands ROGER his notepad and pen.*

ROGER (*to* ANN). I need to look at the tins.

ANN. I'm in charge of the tins.

ROGER. We're only counting them.

GEORGE. To work out rations.

ANN. Allan?

ALLAN. Let them. It's important.

*ROGER and GEORGE count the tins and check the labels for amounts. They do a quick head count as well.*

Wait – there's still something else.

*ALLAN pulls out a second crumpled sail. There is a frightened boy behind it. Everyone turns to look.*

ALFIE. Oh my God.

MARGOT. That's blasphemy.

SAM. Is it a person?

ENID. It's a boy.

ANN. Is he dead?

ALLAN *drags him out – a small boy with red hair, smaller than the rest of them.*

GEORGE. His eyes are open.

MARGARET. That means he's alive.

ALLAN. Certainly is. Hello little 'un.

ANTHEA. A stowaway!

ANN. He's tiny.

ALLAN. Guess that's how we missed him.

ENID. What's your name then?

*The boy is silent and just looks at them.*

Up you get.

ALFIE. What's wrong with him?

MARGOT. Are you hurt?

MARGARET. Have you hurt yourself?

GEORGE. He's hurt.

SAM. There's no blood.

ARCHIE. If he was hurt he'd c-cry.

SAM. Make him get up.

ALFIE. Kick him.

ROGER. No!

ALLAN. Come on, mister. Let's get you up and about.

ALLAN *lifts the boy to his feet. The boy stands unsteadily and looks at them all in turn. He sucks his thumb.*

GEORGE. How did he get on the boat?

ALFIE. Tie him up and let's interrogate him.

SAM. Yeah.

ROGER. There's no need for that.

ENID. Look at his hair.

MARGOT. Red as a little fox!

ALLAN. What's your name then, fella?

ENID. Foxy!

*They laugh*

ALLAN. Well?

MARGARET. Why doesn't he speak?

ENID. Cat got your tongue?

MARGOT. He's frightened.

SAM. He's just pretending.

GEORGE. Was it all the noise? The fire and the smoke? It's over now.

ALFIE. We're all over it. He should be too.

MARGARET. He should be thankful. We got him out of that hole.

ENID. Say thank you.

ARCHIE. You c-could have starved in there.

MARGOT. Say it to God at least.

GEORGE. Why don't you speak?

ALFIE. He might be deaf.

SAM. WHY DON'T YOU SPEAK?

ROGER. Stop it.

MARGOT. He might be speaking inside.

SAM. I'll give you a marble if you speak.

ALFIE. You've got marbles?

SAM. Loads.

ALFIE. Let's see.

ANTHEA. I don't like it that he doesn't say anything.

MARGOT. He's scared.

ENID. I think he's rude.

MARGARET. Maybe he saw something.

ANN. Like what?

MARGARET. Something awful.

ANN. What would be so awful someone would stop speaking?

MARGARET. I… I don't know.

GEORGE. Maybe he can write it down instead. Give me my notepad.

ROGER. I'm using it.

SAM. Maybe he doesn't speak English.

ALFIE. Yeah. Maybe – he's an enemy.

*A collective intake of breath.*

Maybe – he sank our ship.

ALLAN. Enemies speak English too.

SAM. Are you? Are you an enemy?

ALFIE. Tie him up.

ALLAN. He looks English.

ANN. How?

ALLAN. His hair.

ANN. Red? That's Scottish.

ALLAN. Scottish then.

ENID. He might be Irish.

ROGER. So? They're all allies.

ALFIE. Well that depends.

SAM. On what?

ALFIE. On where you live. My uncle lives near the border and he had to fight some Scottish.

GEORGE. Why?

ALFIE. They wanted his house.

SAM. Why?

ALFIE. It was near a river. He had to kill them.

ANTHEA. Everyone fights. It doesn't mean anything.

ROGER. Can everyone be quiet? I'm trying to concentrate. (*On working out the rations.*)

GEORGE. What's that round his neck?

SAM. It's a torch.

ALFIE. Let's see.

GEORGE. I saw it first.

ARCHIE. Does it w-work?

ROGER. Leave it – it's his.

GEORGE *grabs it and switches it on. It works.*

MARGOT. It's a miracle.

ALFIE. Pfff, hardly.

ENID. We can signal for help.

ALLAN (*firmly*). No. Signalling can attract the enemy.

ANTHEA. Still, hooray for Foxy!

ROGER. That's not his name.

ALFIE. What for?

ANTHEA. For bringing us a torch.

ANN. What is his name then?

GEORGE. Foxy.

MARGOT. Foxy Loxy.

ENID. Nasty Foxy.

ANTHEA. Will he make the sky fall on our heads?

ALFIE. Foxes are vermin. They kill chickens.

ALLAN. He's shivering. Soaking. We need to get him some dry clothes.

ALFIE. There aren't any.

ALLAN. Each of us donate one piece of clothing each.

ROGER. Good idea.

ALFIE. No it isn't.

GEORGE. I'm wet too.

SAM. And me. I don't get special treatment.

MARGARET. Foxy's a boy. Boys don't wear girls' clothes.

ENID. Depends…

MARGOT. Don't be silly.

ALLAN. Alright. Boys only then.

*The boys look at* ALLAN. *They don't want to do it.*

I'll start. He can have my jumper.

ANN. Are you sure?

ALLAN. It's only till his is dry. Then we'll swap back.

ALLAN *strips* FOXY *to the waist then takes off his own jumper and puts it on* FOXY. *It is way too big.* ALLAN *lays out Foxy's wet clothes so they can dry.*

ARCHIE. It's t-too big.

ALFIE. He looks silly.

ALLAN. It doesn't matter. You next. Archie, wasn't it?

ARCHIE. Yes. He can have my g-gloves.

ALLAN. Good lad. Roger?

ROGER. He can borrow my shoes.

ANN. Roger already gave his shirt to Anthea.

ROGER. That's alright, I don't mind.

ALLAN. Thank you, Roger, very kind. Sam?

SAM. He can have a marble.

ALLAN. That won't keep him warm. Give him your pyjama bottoms.

SAM. Oh but –

ALLAN. Just till he stops shivering.

SAM. What about me? *I'll* be cold.

MARGARET. Foxy's smaller.

ALLAN. That's right. It's the right thing to do.

MARGOT. It's the *Christian* thing to do.

ENID. That's right.

ALLAN. It's the human thing to do.

SAM. Then turn around. All of you.

*They avert their eyes.* SAM *grumbles, takes off his shorts and sulkily hands them over.*

ALLAN. That's very charitable, thank you, Sam. George?

GEORGE. I gave my jumper to Anthea.

ALLAN. Then give him something else.

ANN. George has given enough.

ALFIE. Yeah he's done his bit.

ALLAN. You'll get it back.

GEORGE. He can have my torch.

ALLAN. That was his anyway.

GEORGE. My hat then.

ALLAN. Alright.

ANTHEA. What about Alfie?

ALFIE. What about him?

ANTHEA. You've not given anything.

ALFIE. How about I not punch him?

ROGER (*looking up from his calculations*). Stop that, there'll be no punching.

ALFIE. I know. That's my contribution.

*They stand and look at* FOXY *in everyone else's clothes.*

He looks ridiculous.

ENID. He should be grateful.

ANTHEA. Say thank you.

FOXY *sits down and curls his legs up under his chin.*

ENID. So rude.

ROGER (*of his calculations*). Bugger.

GEORGE. What?

ROGER. I'm going to have to recalculate the rations. I just did it with twelve of us and then he turned up.

ENID. Another mouth to feed.

ANN. Oh my God.

ALLAN. What?

ANN. We're thirteen.

ENID. So?

ANN. There's thirteen of us. That's bad luck.

ALFIE. Oh yeah.

ROGER. It doesn't matter.

ANN. It does.

MARGARET. Does it?

SAM. Why?

ALLAN. No it doesn't.

ROGER. Yeah it's silly.

MARGOT. What about Friday the thirteenth?

ANTHEA. Bad luck isn't real.

ANN. Of course it is, it happens all the time.

ALFIE. Yeah, look around you.

MARGOT. Enid drew a circle.

MARGARET. So?

MARGOT. That was for *good* luck.

ALFIE. Didn't work, did it? He turned up.

ANN. And now we're thirteen.

ANTHEA. Thirteen's just a number.

MARGOT. How come good luck is real but bad luck isn't?

ALFIE. One more mouth to feed is what matters.

SAM. Yeah that's right. Less for the rest.

ARCHIE. We could p-put him back.

GEORGE. Yeah, under the sail. Forget all about him.

ANN. We'd still be thirteen.

ALFIE. Chuck him in then.

ALLAN. Stop that. He's here now and he's one of us. Survivors, remember?

ROGER. Yeah, survivors.

ALL (*less enthusiastic than before*). Survivors.

ALLAN. Right. We need to start rowing.

*Collective grumbles: 'Oh really?', 'But they're so heavy', 'I hate rowing', 'I don't know how'.*

Twelve of us, four oars, that's three to an oar.

SAM. What about Foxy?

ALLAN. He's warming up, he can join in later.

ALFIE. He's too puny, he won't be any use.

MARGOT. I'm still warming up.

MARGARET. And me. How come Foxy gets to sit out?

ENID. What about Amy?

ANTHEA. Amy's sick.

AMY. I'm fine.

ANTHEA. No you're not.

ENID. So it's eleven of us. On four oars.

SAM. What does that make it?

ENID. Four into eleven doesn't go.

ALFIE. So we've all got to do more work cos of those two?

GEORGE. Rubbish.

SAM. Yeah, rubbish.

ROGER. Stop moaning and get on with it.

*In different groups of two and three they each get hold of an oar.*

Right. Which direction should we row in?

SAM. Good point.

ARCHIE. I've got a c-compass.

ALLAN. Have you?

ARCHIE. In the handle of my p-penknife.

ALFIE. You've got a penknife?

ARCHIE. Only a s-small one.

SAM. You never said.

ROGER. Let's see.

ALFIE. Nice one.

ARCHIE. Sheffield steel.

SAM. Nice.

ALFIE. Do they still make that?

ARCHIE. It's an old one. But still the best. My dad says.

ALFIE. That's cos it's sharpest.

ALLAN. Which way is east?

GEORGE *checks the sun and* ARCHIE *his penknife compass.*

GEORGE. Over there.

ARCHIE. Yep.

ANN. Why east?

ALLAN. Back to England.

ANN. Well let's get going then.

ROGER. Done it!

ENID. Done what?

ROGER. The sum.

ANN. What sum?

ROGER. For the rations.

ANN. Oh.

ROGER. Right, so there's six tins of biscuits, twenty biscuits per tin.

ANN. Do we have to do this now?

ALLAN. It's important.

ROGER. Six tins of ham, fifteen slices in each. And six tins of water, one and a half litres in each. If we say three biscuits is a meal, and three meals per day, then we have enough for everyone until… tomorrow morning.

ANN. What?

ALFIE. Is that all?

ROGER. But wait, there's also the ham. There's just under seven slices each.

MARGARET. They're wafer thin.

SAM. Yeah, ham doesn't fill you up.

ALLAN. Water's most important.

GEORGE. Yeah, you die without water.

ROGER. Well in that case there's… six hundred and ninety-two mill each.

ALFIE. That's like… a large glass.

ROGER. Or two small glasses.

ALLAN. It's about a pint.

ANTHEA. Amy should get more.

ALFIE. No way.

ANTHEA. She's hurt.

AMY. I'm fine.

ANTHEA. No you're not.

ROGER. I mean per person.

ANN. That's not nearly enough!

MARGARET. We're doomed!

ROGER. But it's enough for today, and we'll be rescued tomorrow.

ALFIE. We'd bloody better be.

SAM. I can't see anyone yet.

ALLAN. Give them a chance. We'll have drifted.

ARCHIE. What if it's l-longer?

ROGER. It won't be.

ANN. How do you know?

ALLAN. We're kids. They won't just leave us here.

*They look out.*

Better get rowing.

ENID. Rowing makes you thirsty.

ALLAN. Slowly then.

DAY ONE 57

MARGARET. I'm scared.

MARGOT. Me too.

SAM. Shut up.

MARGARET. You shut up.

ALLAN. We're survivors, remember? We'll survive.

ROGER. Think of it as an adventure.

ENID. A horrid one.

ALLAN. Someone needs to count.

ANN. Count what?

ALLAN. Time. For the rowing.

MARGOT. I'll do it.

> MARGOT *scampers to the prow.* ALLAN *and* ANN *have a hushed conversation.*

ANN (*quiet, to* ALLAN). We need to keep count of more than just rowing. Three cups of water each, I make it.

ALLAN. Per day?

ANN. In total.

ALLAN. It's fine.

ANN. It's not fine, Allan. Not fine at all.

ALLAN. Every man for himself.

ANN. I thought we were sticking together?

ALLAN. We are.

ANN. Make your mind up.

ALLAN. What's the difference? If everyone looks out for themselves, we'll all stick together. Right?

ANN (*hesitant*)....Right.

ALLAN. Survivors.

ANN. Survivors.

MARGOT. One-two. One-two. One-two. One-two.

*Everyone joins in with the 'One-two'.*

*With considerable effort on the heavy oars, they start to row. The mist descends and the boat disappears from view.*

*Darkness falls.*

**Day Two**

*The mist parts and the lifeboat fades into view. It is a hive of early-morning activity on board. Seagulls caw above. In quieter moments during this opening, a faint yelping noise can be heard, like a distressed puppy.*

*The children play in pairs at different points around the boat:*

ANTHEA *tends to* AMY, *checking her wounds and changing her bandages as necessary.*

ANN *prepares breakfast.*

ENID *is inspecting her own hands, which are raw and bleeding from rowing.*

ALFIE *is showing* ALLAN *his catapult.*

ARCHIE *and* GEORGE *are threading together a piece of string and an unfolded paperclip to make a fishing line and hook.*

SAM *and* ROGER *are seeing how far they can throw some of* SAM's *marbles overboard.* SAM *also spits. Eventually* ALFIE *notices and goes over to suggest loading his catapult with marbles, which they do. They fire some into the sea, with surprising force.*

MARGOT *and* MARGARET *play a clapping game and chant a rhyme:*

MARGOT / MARGARET.
Teddy Bear, Teddy Bear,
Turn around.
Teddy Bear, Teddy Bear,
Touch the ground.

Teddy Bear, Teddy Bear
Touch your shoe.
Teddy Bear, Teddy Bear
That will do.
Teddy Bear, Teddy Bear,
Go upstairs.
Teddy Bear, Teddy Bear,
Say your prayers.
Teddy Bear, Teddy Bear,
Turn out the light.
Teddy Bear, Teddy Bear,
Say goodnight!

ENID *whimpers and looks around for what to do to stop the pain in her hands. Eventually she decides to lean overboard and dip them in the sea. As soon as she does so she screams. The salt in her wounds is unbearable; she screams and screams.*

ENID. Ow ow ow ow ow!

ROGER *rushes over to her.*

ROGER. What is it?

ENID. My hands, my hands!

ROGER. Show me.

ENID. I put them in the sea and now they're burning!

ROGER. Come here.

ENID. Make it stop!

*Chorus of murmuring from the others. 'What's going on?', 'What's all the racket?' 'Is she hurt?', etc.*

ROGER. It's the salt water in the cuts. Here.

ROGER *finds some drinking water and pours some onto* ENID's *hands.*

ENID. Ow ow ow ow ow!

ROGER. Hold still, this will wash the salt out.

ANN. Hey!

ENID. Oh God, oh God, oh God.

ROGER. Better?

ENID. They're bleeding.

ANN (*to* ALLAN). That's drinking water.

ANTHEA. Awful. Don't look. (*Covers* AMY*'s eyes.*)

ALFIE. It's good if it bleeds. Washes the salt out.

ALLAN *marches over, furious.*

ALLAN. That's drinking water!

ALFIE. Yeah!

SAM. Yeah, what are you doing?

ENID. It was Roger.

ROGER. It's only a bit.

ALLAN. You're wasting it!

ROGER. She's hurt.

ENID. It's from too much rowing. You made us!

ALLAN (*of the water tin*). Give that to me.

ROGER *hands it over.*

(*To* ENID.) That was your ration for the day.

ENID. No!

ROGER. That's not fair.

MARGARET. Lick it up then.

ALFIE. Yeah it's not coming out of my ration.

SAM. Nor mine.

MARGARET. Nor mine.

GEORGE. No way.

MARGOT. Allan's right, you don't waste water. It's a crime.

ROGER (*to* ENID). You can share mine.

ENID. Thank you.

ALLAN. I'll need to recalculate. Give me the pad.

ANN. Idiot.

ALLAN (*to* ENID). I hope your hands drop off.

ROGER. Allan –

ALLAN. What?

*ENID bursts into tears.*

ENID. I'm sorry.

ROGER. It's alright, he didn't mean it.

*ALLAN does some more arithmetic in the pad, adjusting ROGER's sums from yesterday.*

GEORGE. It's okay, we're being rescued today.

ARCHIE. How d-do you know?

GEORGE. They said so yesterday.

MARGARET. Well where are they then?

ANTHEA. It's still morning. Maybe they're coming later.

MARGOT. I can't see anyone.

SAM. Same as yesterday – nothing as far you can see.

GEORGE. They might be just over the horizon.

ALFIE. And what if they're not?

ALLAN (*of the sum*). Just let me do this.

ANTHEA. Can we have breakfast yet?

ANN. Not yet. Allan's working it out.

ANTHEA. Amy needs water.

ALLAN. Just – hold on.

ANTHEA. Her lips are dry.

MARGARET. Everyone's lips are dry.

ANTHEA. It's different for invalids.

ALLAN (*firmly*). She'll wait her turn, like everyone else.

*ANTHEA backs down. In the background, FOXY starts to yelp.*

GEORGE. I'm hungry.

ARCHIE. I'm c-cold.

MARGOT. I didn't sleep.

ROGER. Just, be patient. We'll be rescued soon.

MARGARET. When?

ROGER. I don't know.

ALFIE. Nobody knows!

ROGER. It could be tomorrow now.

ENID. That's what you said yesterday.

ANN. It could be never.

ROGER. Don't say that!

ANN. Well we are cursed – thirteen.

ROGER. Shut up.

ALLAN. They won't just leave us.

ANTHEA. What if they can't see us?

ALLAN. Tie my scarf.

ROGER. To what?

ALLAN. An oar. Hold it up.

ENID. Then what?

ALLAN. Wave it.

*They tie* ALLAN's *scarf to an oar.*

ANTHEA. Careful of Amy!

ALFIE. Always in the way.

*They start to shout, and splash the oars. Someone waves the makeshift flag,* ALLAN *goes back to his calculations.*

SAM. We can drum!

GEORGE. How?

SAM. On a tin.

MARGARET. Brilliant idea!

MARGOT. With what?

SAM. The tin opener?

ANN. No. It's too precious.

SAM. A marble?

ALFIE. My catapult.

ANN. Yes – both of those. Anything.

*SAM and ALFIE start to drum on an upturned tin with a marble and ALFIE's catapult. They all drum on anything to hand.*

ALLAN. Quiet! I can't concentrate!

SAM. We won't be spotted otherwise!

MARGOT. Oh, it's no use!

ENID. Yes, we're miles from anywhere.

ARCHIE. This is a w-waste of energy.

MARGOT. I'm thirsty.

GEORGE. I was thirsty before.

SAM. Now I'm thirstier.

MARGARET. Are we going to die?

ALLAN. Don't say that! Nobody is ever to say that. Do you understand?

*Pause.*

MARGOT. Is it because we're cursed?

ARCHIE. Why are we c-cursed?

MARGOT. Because we're thirteen.

ROGER. That's ridiculous.

MARGARET. Then why haven't we been rescued?

ALLAN. It's only been a day.

MARGOT. Two days.

ROGER. Today's hardly started.

MARGOT. I don't want us to be thirteen.

ANN. Neither do I.

ROGER. Well there's nothing we can do about it.

ALFIE. Yes there is.

SAM. What?

ROGER. No there isn't.

SAM. What can we do?

ROGER. We can stick together, that's what.

ANN. Every man for himself.

ROGER. No –

ANN. Yes, it's the same. If we all look out for ourselves, we'll all be okay.

ROGER. That's stupid.

GEORGE. Why is thirteen bad luck?

ROGER. It isn't.

ANN. It is.

ANTHEA. My mum thinks it is.

ROGER. Well she's wrong.

ANTHEA. She's a nurse.

ARCHIE. My b-brother does too.

ENID. And my aunt.

ROGER. Well then she's silly.

ARCHIE. They can't all be silly.

ENID. My aunt won't go out on Friday the thirteenth.

SAM. That's because it's a Friday too.

ENID. So thirteen on its own –

ROGER. Doesn't mean anything.

GEORGE. So why is it unlucky?

ROGER. It's not.

MARGOT. It is. It's because it's from the Bible. At the Last Supper, the thirteenth was Judas, and he betrayed Jesus.

ALFIE. Superstition.

MARGARET. I'm scared.

ANN. We'll get through this.

ENID. How?

ANN. We will.

MARGOT. How?

ROGER. By sticking together, that's how.

ALLAN. It's not that there's thirteen of us, it's that there's too many of us.

SAM. Can we eat yet?

ALLAN. Well, I've recalculated all the rations over three days.

ENID. Three?

ALFIE. Three whole days?

ALLAN. That's worst case.

ROGER. We'll easily be rescued by then.

SAM. We'll be starving by then!

ALLAN. We'll all be hungry. And thirsty. But if we stick to this, some of us might just make it.

MARGARET. Some of us?

ROGER. And once we get rescued we can eat and drink the lot.

ALLAN. Well, there won't be any left.

ROGER. On the rescue ship.

MARGOT. Like a feast!

ROGER. Exactly.

SAM. I'd love a feast.

MARGARET. A cake.

GEORGE. Chips!

ALFIE. A nice juicy steak.

ANTHEA. I just want some water.

ALLAN. Here's how it's got to work. We've finished the ham.

ALFIE. What, all of it?

GEORGE. No way!

ALLAN. There was only six tins. That's ninety slices. Roger?

ROGER. He's right.

ALLAN. We said seven slices each yesterday, which used it all up.

ENID. Well I didn't have any – I'm vegetarian.

ANTHEA. How stupid to eat it all.

SAM. We thought we'd be rescued, didn't we?

ALLAN. So these new rations are for biscuits and water only, over three days.

ROGER. At least there's still some of those left.

ANN. Listen to Allan.

ALLAN. There was six tins of biscuits. That's one hundred and twenty. We had six each yesterday, so there's forty-eight left.

MARGOT. You're clever.

MARGARET. Only forty-eight?

MARGOT. Allan's clever.

ANN. That's why he's the leader.

ENID. We had over half the biscuits yesterday?

ALFIE. Two-thirds.

ENID. Oh my God.

ALLAN. Forty-eight divided by thirteen people, divided by three days… is one and a quarter biscuits each per day.

ARCHIE. Per d-day?

ENID. Per whole day?

SAM. No way.

ALFIE. Forget it.

MARGARET. That's not going to work.

ANTHEA. Amy should get more.

ALFIE. Amy can piss off.

ROGER. What about Foxy?

ALFIE. Him too.

ENID. He doesn't need food, he doesn't row.

ANN. What about water?

ALLAN. Well, there's six tins of one and a half litres. We drank half yesterday.

ENID. Half the water?

SAM. Oh my God.

ANN. Well there *are* thirteen of us.

ALFIE (*to* ENID). And you put some on your hands? You idiot.

ENID. Get lost.

ROGER. Hey, I did – not her.

ALFIE. Then you're a stupid idiot too.

ANN. Stop that. How much is left?

ALLAN. Four and a half litres, divided by thirteen people, divided by three days…

MARGOT. Oh why are we thirteen?!

ALLAN. ...equals one hundred and fifteen mill each.

ANN. Per day?

ALLAN. Per day.

ALFIE. That's nothing!

SAM. That's half a cup.

MARGARET (*i.e.* ENID's). Does that include hers?

ALLAN. Yes.

MARGARET. Cos she wasted hers.

MARGOT. That's it on the floor.

ENID. Shut up.

ANN. We can't deny her a ration.

ENID. That's right, you can't.

ALLAN. Why not?

ANN. Allan!

ALLAN. What? It was her fault.

ROGER. It was *my* fault.

ALFIE. Both of you then. All the more for us.

ENID. I DIDN'T EVEN HAVE ANY HAM!

ANTHEA. We can't think like this!

ALFIE. Why not?

ARCHIE. We're all r-responsible for ourselves.

ALLAN. That's right. If everyone looks out for themselves we'll all be fine. Logical.

GEORGE. Logical.

ROGER. Stupid.

ALFIE. In that case I'll have what I like.

ANTHEA. What about Amy?

ENID. What about her?

ANTHEA. She's sick, she needs more.

ALFIE. Well there isn't any more.

ANTHEA. I mean more than the rest.

ALFIE. THERE ISN'T ANY MORE.

ALLAN. Calm down.

ENID. She's not having mine.

SAM. Or mine.

MARGOT. Or mine.

ROGER. Let's recalculate over two days.

ANN. Yes let's do that.

ALLAN. Well –

ALFIE. Or we could just help ourselves.

ROGER. No one's doing that.

ALFIE. Oh yeah? Who's going to stop it?

ANN. I've got the tin opener.

ALFIE. Then you'd better give it here.

ANN. Or what?

ALLAN. Sit down, Alfie.

ALFIE. I'm not sitting down for anyone.

*Tense pause. It is interrupted by a yelping noise.*

GEORGE. What's that noise?

ENID. What noise?

GEORGE. A yelping noise.

SAM. It's from over there.

*They look around and find* FOXY *under the prow.*

Foxy.

*They drag him out.*

GEORGE. Were you asleep?

ALFIE. Lazy sod.

SAM. He was yelping in his sleep.

GEORGE. Like a dog.

SAM. Bad dream, was it?

GEORGE. You're safe now.

ENID. Eurgh look!

SAM. What?

ENID. He's wet himself!

MARGARET. Eurgh!

MARGOT. Eurgh!

SAM. Eurgh!

ALFIE. Dirty little sod.

ANN. It's dripping on the deck.

ANTHEA. All down his pyjamas.

SAM. They're *my* bloody pyjamas!

ARCHIE. And my g-gloves

ALLAN. And my jumper!

GEORGE. And my hat!

SAM. Get them off him!

GEORGE, ALFIE, ARCHIE, ALLAN *and* SAM *pile onto* FOXY *and strip him of all their clothes.*

ROGER. Careful!

SAM. They're ruined.

ALLAN. Disgusting.

ANTHEA. Dunk them in the water.

SAM. Dunk *him* in the water.

MARGARET. Dirty little grub.

ANTHEA. He didn't mean it, he just had a bad dream.

MARGOT (*to* SAM). You said bloody.

SAM. Yes I bloody did. What are you gonna do about it?

MARGARET. Put Foxy in the toilet bucket!

ALL (*except* ROGER). Yeah!

SAM. Put the bucket on his head!

ALL (*except* ROGER). Yeah!

ROGER (*with force*). No!

*Pause.*

You'll do no such thing. Do you hear me?

ALLAN. Empty it.

SAM. Yeah. Make yourself useful at least.

*They pass the bucket down from one end of the boat to the other, holding their noses.* ALFIE *can't resist taking a peek.*

ALFIE. Eurgh!

*The boys laugh.*

*The bucket reaches* FOXY's *end.* ROGER *stows it under the stern.*

ROGER. Sorry, little man. You'll have to take good care of it for us.

ALLAN. He can empty it.

SAM. Yeah that can be his job.

ENID. Yes, he should do *something*.

ALFIE. Think you can manage that?

FOXY *is shivering in just his underpants and Roger's shoes, given to him in the previous scene.*

ROGER (*gently*). Come on, fella. Let's get your old things back on.

ANN. Breakfast!

> ROGER *and* ANTHEA *help get* FOXY *dressed.*
>
> ANN *doles out breakfast* (*one biscuit each*) *and water* (*half a cup*). *Everyone lines up to receive theirs in silence.*
>
> ALLAN *and* ROGER *are last.*
>
> Wash your hands first.

ROGER. Why?

ANN. You touched Foxy.

ROGER. Where?

ANN. Overboard.

> ROGER *rinses his hands in the sea.*
>
> ALLAN *takes his biscuit and drinks his water.*
>
> ROGER *is last. He downs his water and holds out the cup for more.*
>
> That's your lot.

ROGER. For Foxy.

ALLAN. He's had his.

ROGER. No he hasn't.

ALLAN. He has.

ROGER. When?

ALLAN. Well he's not getting any.

ROGER. Why not?

ALLAN. Because of what he did.

ROGER. What did he do?

ALLAN. Wet himself.

ROGER. That wasn't his fault.

ALLAN. Whose fault was it then?

ROGER. He didn't mean to.

ALLAN. But he did it.

ROGER. He's thirsty.

ALLAN. How do you know?

ROGER. He hasn't drunk anything.

ALLAN. He hasn't said he's thirsty.

ROGER. Of course he is. We all are.

ALLAN. Foxy, are you thirsty?

*FOXY shivers silently in his underpants.*

See? Not thirsty.

ROGER (*of the water tin*). Give that here.

*ANN holds it away.*

MARGOT. He can drink sea water.

ENID. Or suck his shorts!

ALFIE. Yeah, make him suck his own wee!

MARGARET. Dirty little git.

ROGER. He has the right to his fair share.

ENID. Less for him is more for us.

ALLAN. That's right.

ROGER. Ann?

*Pause.*

ANN. No. We must stick together.

ALFIE. You mean die together. Why are we bothering?

ROGER. Bothering with what?

ALFIE. Feeding these two.

GEORGE. Which?

ALFIE. Foxy and Amy. Look at them. They're both useless.

ANTHEA. Amy's sick!

ROGER. Stop this now. Ann?

ANN. Alright, let's just –

ALLAN. I'm with Alfie.

ANN. What?

ALLAN. Who votes to stop giving Foxy and Amy food and water –

ROGER. No!

ALLAN. – and having it ourselves instead?

ANN. Allan!

ALLAN. Every man for himself. You said so yourself.

ANN. I didn't mean –

ENID. I do.

MARGOT. I do.

MARGARET. I do.

ROGER. I don't.

ANN. Alright, stop this, all of you.

ROGER. Yes, there's no need.

ENID. There is.

ROGER. We'll be rescued!

MARGOT. When?

ROGER. Any day now!

MARGARET. Any day?

ROGER. Any hour – any minute.

SAM. Where are they then?

ALFIE. Are they coming up in a submarine?

ENID. Yeah, are they right underneath us?

GEORGE. I don't think so.

ROGER. Tomorrow then.

MARGOT. That's what you said yesterday.

ROGER. Allan?

ALLAN. I don't know. All I know is – is that everyone should take responsibility for themselves.

ANN. Does that mean sharing?

ALLAN. It means… making sure you're alright. For the good of everyone. No one should be a burden.

*Pause.*

ANN. Well, alright.

ROGER. So does that mean Foxy can have –

ALLAN. Except Foxy.

ROGER. No.

ANTHEA. No.

ENID. Yes.

ALLAN. Yes.

ANN. That settles it.

ALFIE. We may as well just get rid of him now.

*ALFIE makes a move towards* FOXY.

ROGER. Don't you dare.

ANN. Yes, let's just leave it.

*ROGER scoops* FOXY *up and takes him to one end of the boat.*

*The two of them momentarily disappear from view behind the sail where the toilet bucket is.*

ALFIE *follows.*

Alfie…

ALFIE *gets his catapult out.*

ALFIE (*to* SAM). Marble.

*SAM gives ALFIE a marble.*

ANN. Alfie, what did I say?

ALFIE *loads the marble.*

Alfie, no!

ALFIE *fires behind the sail. A voice cries out.*

ROGER *stumbles out, clutching his head. Blood trickles between his fingers. He collapses.*

*Some of the girls scream.*

MARGARET. Oh my God.

ANTHEA. Oh no.

MARGOT. Oh God please.

ENID. Blood.

ANTHEA. Help him.

ANTHEA *goes to him.*

ARCHIE. You stupid b-bastard.

ENID. What have you done?

ALLAN. You bully!

ALFIE. You told me to!

ALLAN. No I didn't!

ANN. Give that to me.

ANN *snatches* ALFIE's *catapult.*

Is he alright?

ANTHEA. Not really.

ALLAN. Is he – Will he –

ANTHEA. I don't know.

ALLAN. You're a nurse.

ANTHEA. No I'm not.

ROGER *groans.*

Alright, it's alright. I need more bandages.

ALLAN (*to* ALFIE). Take off your shirt.

ALFIE. Take yours off.

ALLAN. Take it off.

> ALFIE *does so.* ALLAN *tears it.* ANTHEA *uses the strips to bandage* ROGER*'s head.* ALLAN *and* ANN *whisper.*

ANTHEA. It's swelling.

ALFIE. He'll be fine.

ANTHEA. Shut up.

SAM. It was my smallest marble.

ANTHEA. Shut up, both of you. (*To* GEORGE.) Take Amy, and Foxy, their biscuit and water.

> GEORGE *does so.* ANN *allows it.* ENID *stands and attempts to speak with authority.*

ENID. There will be nothing more like this. Do you understand? Nothing. We are not savages.

*Pause.* ALLAN *breaks away from whispering with* ANN.

ALLAN. Alright, here's what we're going to do. If we all continue to eat, there isn't going to be enough. But Enid's right, we're not savages. We won't let the strong take from the weak. We need to make the remaining rations do as much good as they can, for all of us, for the group. So tomorrow morning, before breakfast, we will meet again, and we will all make our case.

ENID. What?

SAM. Our case?

MARGARET. Our case for what?

ANN. Our case for rations.

GEORGE. You mean –

ALLAN. Why any of us should get anything at all.

MARGARET. How do you mean?

ALLAN. Maybe you've got a useful skill – like, like, you're the leader. Or, or you can shout loudly, or row hard, or, or, maybe you're just a good person. But you have something which is of benefit to the group. A reason for your rations. George will write them all down. And then… then we'll decide.

ALFIE. Decide what?

ALLAN. Which of us are going to stick together.

MARGARET. What happens to the others?

ALLAN. For those left over… it's every man for himself.

*Whimpering among them all.*

You have the rest of today to think about what you'll say.

ANN. Now let's row.

MARGARET. Rowing's a waste of time.

SAM. A waste of energy.

GEORGE. Yeah.

ARCHIE. Yeah.

ALLAN. Well what else can we do? Give up?

*Murmurs of 'No, Allan.'*

We either row, or we die. And none of us want to die, right?

*Murmurs of 'No, Allan.'*

Survivors!

ALL (*wearily*). Survivors.

ALLAN. So let's row.

ALFIE. Where to?

ALLAN. To the end.

*Those who can all take an oar and* MARGOT *scampers to the prow to count.*

MARGOT. One-two. One-two.

ALL. One-two. One-two.

*Fog descends, obscuring the boat from view.*

## Day Three

*The mist parts and the boat fades into view.*

*The group has fractured into several smaller groups:*

ALLAN *and* ANN *open tins guardedly, whispering and looking over their shoulders.*

MARGARET *and* MARGOT *do Cat's Cradle with string.*

GEORGE *helps* ANTHEA *tend to* AMY *and the injured* ROGER, *who is now lying down next to* AMY *with a bandage round his head.*

SAM *and* ARCHIE *arm wrestle.* ARCHIE *is stronger and keeps winning.*

ALFIE *practises aiming his catapult at seagulls overhead, though he has nothing to load it with.*

ENID *rows on her own.*

ALLAN. How are your hands?

ANN. Fine.

ALLAN. Let's see.

ANN. I'm not so thin-skinned.

ALLAN (*taking her hands*). Soft though.

ANN. I rowed a lot on my uncle's estate.

ALLAN. Where's that?

ANN. Buckinghamshire. A beautiful big mansion surrounded by oak trees.

ALLAN. It sounds lovely.

ANN. It was. I always said I'd get married there.

ALLAN. And did you?

ANN. I'm thirteen.

ALLAN. I'd marry you. You're beautiful.

*ANN is shy and doesn't know what to say.*

We could go back to your uncle's estate.

ANN. It isn't there any more.

ALLAN. What happened?

ANN. We lived there for a while, after the cities died. The lake had fresh water, with rowing boats and black swans.

ALLAN. What happened?

ANN. Then they came for the rural areas too.

*Pause.*

ALLAN. I've never heard of black swans.

ANN. They're from Australia.

ALLAN. How many?

ANN. Lots. I never counted. Sometimes they'd all take off, and it was like a flock of black angels, filling up the sky.

ALLAN. Beautiful.

ANN. And a bit scary too.

ALLAN. I'd like to see that.

ANN. They're all dead now.

ALLAN. Dead?

ANN. Eaten. Used up for food.

ALLAN. Of course.

ANN. That's what they do.

ALLAN. Awful.

ANN. Not really. Just surviving.

ALLAN. Yes. Like us. Will you think about it?

ANN. What?

ALLAN. Marrying me. After this is all over? I could ask your uncle.

ANN. My uncle's dead.

ALLAN. Your dad then.

ANN. Him too.

ALLAN. I'm sorry.

ANN. It doesn't matter. Hardly unusual, is it?

ALLAN. Getting married would be something to look forward to. Something to save us.

*Pause.* ANN *looks up, towards the oar they erected upright yesterday.*

ANN. Your scarf. It's gone.

ALLAN *looks up.*

ALLAN. Maybe we really are cursed.

MARGARET *and* MARGOT *approach* ANN *and* ALLAN.

MARGARET. Excuse me. The bucket is full.

ALLAN. Already?

MARGOT. It's because there's so many of us.

ALLAN. Well empty it then.

MARGARET. No way.

MARGOT. It's disgusting.

ANN. Anyway, that's Foxy's job.

ALLAN. Oh yeah.

MARGARET. Well he hasn't been doing it.

MARGOT. He just sits there.

MARGARET. Yeah, doing nothing.

MARGOT. Wallowing.

MARGARET. Like a pig.

MARGOT. He probably likes it.

MARGARET. Disgusting.

ALLAN. Well make him.

MARGOT. Make him what?

ALLAN. Empty the bucket.

MARGARET. How?

ALLAN. I don't know. Pinch him. He's got to earn his keep.

*MARGARET and MARGOT go over and disturb FOXY, who is behind the sail. He tumbles out.*

MARGARET. Foxy, the bucket's full.

MARGOT. And it's your job to empty it.

MARGARET. Do it or we'll pinch you.

MARGOT. Hard.

MARGARET. Go on then.

*They stand over FOXY and make him empty the bucket overboard.*

MARGOT. Now piss off.

MARGARET. Yes go away. It's rude to watch.

*MARGARET and MARGOT shove FOXY further down the boat and take turns using the toilet bucket behind the sail.*

*ALFIE approaches SAM.*

ALFIE. I need your marbles.

SAM. What for?

ALFIE. Ammo.

SAM. All of them?

ALFIE. Give me ten.

SAM. What can you swap?

ALFIE. How about I don't shoot you?

*SAM counts out ten marbles.*

*ROGER whispers to ANTHEA.*

ANTHEA (*calling to* ENID). Roger says there's no point rowing on your own.

ENID. Why not?

ANTHEA. We'll go in circles.

ENID. At least we're still moving. Easier to spot.

ALLAN. Alright, it's time.

ANN. It's time. Gather round.

ALLAN (*to* GEORGE). We need your notebook.

*Everyone stops what they're doing and gathers round, except* AMY *who shivers where she lies.* ANTHEA *helps* ROGER *to sit up.*

GEORGE *gets his notebook and pencil.*

ANN *and* ALLAN *have made a pile of biscuits and poured some water into the flask cup. They are displayed on upturned tins, like prizes to be won.*

Here's how it's going to work. Everyone must state two reasons why they're valuable to the boat.

ANN. To us all.

ALLAN. That's right.

SAM. Just two?

ANN. Just two.

ALFIE. What if we've got loads of reasons?

GEORGE. Yeah I'm good at lots of things.

ALLAN. Choose two. That way it's fairest.

ANTHEA. Then what?

ANN. Then – choose one person who you think isn't, and give one reason why.

MARGOT. Isn't what?

ANN. Any use.

ENID. Like Foxy.

ANN. It could be anyone.

ALLAN. But you have to say why.

ENID. He's puny.

MARGARET. We haven't started yet.

ANTHEA. This is horrid.

ANN. It's what we agreed.

ANTHEA. I didn't agree.

ROGER (*weakly*). Nor me.

ALFIE. Shut up.

ALLAN. We all agreed.

ANTHEA. When?

ANN. Yesterday.

ALLAN. You had your chance to object and no one did.

ANN. You should all have been thinking about it.

MARGOT. Do we have to do this?

ENID. Yes.

MARGOT. Why?

ALFIE. Because there isn't enough to go around.

ENID. It's horrid but we have to.

ANN. That's right, we've no choice.

SAM. Have we started?

ALLAN. Not yet.

ANN. George will write everything down.

GEORGE. Talk slowly.

ALFIE. Why don't you write quickly?

MARGARET. Then what happens?

ALLAN. Then we'll vote.

MARGOT. Vote for what?

ENID. For who shouldn't get any more food.

ANN. Or water.

ROGER (*weakly*). This is wrong.

ALLAN. It's necessary.

ROGER (*weakly*). This is all wrong.

ANN. We don't have a choice.

ENID. There isn't enough food.

ALLAN. This is the fairest way.

ENID. Look – this is it.

ANN. All of it.

ARCHIE (*of the food on display*). C-careful! What if a wave comes?

ALLAN. It's calm.

SAM. Calm before the storm.

ENID. This is it. Thirty-one and a half biscuits.

ALLAN. And two tins of water.

*Some whimpering.*

SAM. That's nothing.

ALLAN. It's nothing for thirteen.

ANN. It's something for fewer.

ARCHIE. How many f-fewer?

ENID. As many as possible.

ALFIE. You mean as few as possible.

ENID. Yes. So long as I'm one of them.

ALLAN. Quiet! We must do this properly. Solemnly. It's incredibly serious.

ANTHEA. What happens to the losers?

ALLAN. We'll decide that later.

ENID. Yes. More important is to identify the weakest.

ANTHEA. That's not fair!

ENID. It is if they're useless!

ALLAN. I said quiet!

*Pause.*

We must only speak one at a time. We need something to hold.

MARGOT. How do you mean?

ALLAN. To show who can speak.

ENID. To show whose turn it is.

ALLAN. What about the tin opener?

ANN. No. It's too precious. We need it for the unopened water.

ARCHIE. Wh-what about Roger's w-watch?

ALLAN. Good idea.

ROGER *protests, weakly.*

Alfie – take it.

ALFIE *goes to take* ROGER*'s watch.* ROGER *resists.*
ALFIE *gestures for* ARCHIE*'s penknife, who gives it to him.*
ALFIE *uses it to cut the strap of* ROGER*'s watch. He hands the watch to* ALLAN.

Thank you. Whoever is holding this, may speak. No one else.

Ladies first.

SAM. Why not youngest first?

MARGARET. Cos in everything else we're second.

ALLAN *hands the watch to* ANN.

ANN. I'm Ann. I'm second-in-command.

MARGARET. See?

ALLAN. Quiet.

ANN. Thank you, Allan. That means I have to be here for Allan and make decisions with him. And I've got the tin opener.

MARGOT. That's three things.

ENID. Ssh! (*To* ANN.) Who do you nominate?

ANN. Oh yes. (*Pause.*) This is really hard. But I nominate Alfie.

ALFIE. What?

ENID. Shush!

ALFIE. Why?

ANN. Because you're big. So I think you'll be alright.

ALFIE. Not without food and water!

ENID. Silence!

> GEORGE *writes all this down; this continues throughout this scene.* ANN *passes the watch to* ALLAN.

ALLAN. I should get food and water because I'm the oldest. That means I'm most experienced, and I'm the leader so I have to make decisions.

MARGARET. That's –

ANN. Ssh!

ENID. Who do you nominate?

ALLAN. I nominate Foxy or Amy.

MARGARET. That's two.

ALLAN (*quickly*). Foxy because he's useless and Amy because she's dying.

ANTHEA. No she isn't!

ENID. Stop speaking!

ANTHEA. I'm looking after her!

ENID. It isn't your turn!

ANTHEA. She's not going to die – she's not!

ENID. Shut up!

MARGARET. Allan nominated two people!

ALLAN. I'm allowed, I'm the leader!

ANTHEA. Amy's not going to die, I'm taking care of her!

ENID. You can't speak without the watch!

*ALFIE draws his catapult on them all.*

ALFIE. Shut up, all of you!

*This silences them.*

ALLAN. Thank you, Alfie. (*Then, to* GEORGE.) Did you get that?

GEORGE. Yes.

ALLAN. Foxy and Amy. It's the kindest thing. Noble. Giving the rest of us a better chance.

*ALLAN passes the watch to ENID.*

ENID. I'm Enid, I'm third-in-charge, that means I'm third most important plus I'm good at rowing – so good I make my hands bleed –

MARGARET. Yes, your hands bleed and then you use up all the water.

ANN. Ssh!

*MARGARET is about to defend herself but is shushed by one of the others. ANN gestures for ENID to carry on.*

ENID. I nominate Foxy because he doesn't speak or do anything and that's lazy and selfish and rude.

*ENID passes the watch to GEORGE.*

GEORGE. Oh. Um. I – I'm George and I've – I – I can't think of anything.

SAM. Too bad.

ENID. Ssh.

GEORGE. I've got a notepad!

ALFIE. Anyone can have that.

ENID. Ssh! What else?

GEORGE. Um. And – a pencil!

ALFIE. Anyone can have those.

ENID. Shut up.

ALFIE. They're not reasons.

ALLAN. Quiet! Now nominate.

GEORGE. I… I nominate… Foxy because he doesn't speak.

ALLAN. Good.

GEORGE. I'm sorry, Foxy.

*ALLAN points to pass the watch on, GEORGE passes it to ALFIE.*

ALFIE. I'm Alfie. I'm strongest. I've got a catapult. I've already shown I'm not afraid to shoot it. You need me.

ALLAN. Nominate.

ALFIE. I nominate Archie.

ARCHIE. Wh-what?

ALFIE. Because of his stupid stutter.

ARCHIE. That's n-not fair!

ALFIE (*mocking*). N – n – n!

ALLAN. Anyone can nominate anyone.

ALFIE. Sick of hearing it.

ANTHEA. It's not his fault!

ENID. Quiet, unless you've got the watch!

*ALFIE passes the watch to MARGOT.*

MARGOT. I'm Margot. I believe in Jesus Chris our Lord and Saviour and that makes me a good person. And I'm small and I don't cost much to keep alive.

ENID. Nominate.

MARGOT. I nominate… my dolly Lilly.

SAM. What?

MARGOT. Because she doesn't need food or water so she'll be alright.

ALFIE. That doesn't count.

ALLAN. That's right, it doesn't. You have to nominate a real person or there's no point.

*Pause.*

MARGOT. Alfie.

ALFIE. What?

ALLAN. Say why.

MARGOT. Because he's a bully!

ALFIE. No I'm not –

ENID. Silence!

MARGOT *passes the watch to* SAM.

SAM. I'm Sam. I've got marbles and I'm strong and clever and know how to spit.

MARGARET. That's no use.

ENID. Ssh! Nominate.

SAM. I nominate Foxy and Amy and Archie.

ARCHIE. What?

GEORGE. That's three!

ALLAN. Choose one.

SAM. Archie.

ARCHIE. What – why?

SAM. Because he's got a penknife but he's too afraid to use it.

ARCHIE. No I'm not!

ALFIE. You are. I should have it.

SAM. I should.

ALFIE. I should.

ALLAN. Alright, enough.

SAM *passes the watch to* MARGARET.

MARGARET. I'm Margaret and I've got a little sister back home who needs me to look after her.

GEORGE. So have I!

MARGOT. You've had your turn!

ALFIE. Yours is dead anyway.

GEORGE. Don't say that!

ENID. Quiet!

ALFIE. She didn't make it onto the boat.

ALLAN. Silence!

*Pause.*

Nominate.

MARGARET. Foxy.

ENID. Why?

MARGARET. Because he wet himself.

ANN. Pass it on.

MARGARET *passes the watch to* ANTHEA.

ANTHEA. This is horrible and I don't agree with it.

ANN. You have to say.

ANTHEA. No.

ALLAN. You have to. Why you?

*Pause.*

ANTHEA (*of* AMY *and* ROGER). Because I'm looking after these two.

ENID. But if they weren't here –

ANTHEA. Then neither would I be!

*Pause.*

ALLAN. Nominate.

ANTHEA. I can't.

ENID. You must.

ANTHEA. I can't.

*Pause.*

Myself.

GEORGE. What?

SAM. She can't do that.

MARGARET. That's not allowed.

MARGOT. Is that allowed?

ALFIE. I don't see why not. Allan?

ALLAN. It's not exactly looking out for yourself but I suppose it'll do.

ALFIE. All the more for the rest of us.

ARCHIE. You have to s-say why.

ANTHEA. Because everything else is horrible!

ANTHEA *passes the watch to* ROGER, *who holds it tight and mumbles something inaudible.*

ALLAN. Not him.

SAM. Why not?

ALLAN. He's injured.

ANN. They still get a vote.

ENID. What's he saying?

ROGER. No.

ANTHEA. He doesn't agree with it.

ALLAN. He has to nominate.

ROGER *shakes his head.*

Give us the watch then.

ROGER *holds it tight in a fist.*

(*To* ALFIE.) Get it off him.

ALFIE *climbs on top of* ROGER *and tries to prise his fist open to get the watch.* ROGER *moans and cries out.*

ALFIE. Let go. Let go of it!

ROGER *holds on tight.*

(*To* ARCHIE.) Use your penknife.

ARCHIE. W-what?

ALFIE. Cut his fingers off.

*The girls gasp and scream, some whisper 'No!'* ANN *considers intervening but* ALLAN *holds her back.*

(*To* ARCHIE.) Do it!

ARCHIE *dithers.* ALFIE *grabs his penknife and moves to cut* ROGER. ROGER*'s fist springs open and he offers up the watch.* ALFIE *takes it.*

(*To* SAM, *of* ARCHIE.) You were right. Gutless.

ALFIE *hands* ARCHIE *back his penknife, aggressively.* ARCHIE *tries not to cry.*

(*To* ALLAN, *of the watch.*) Who's next?

ENID. Archie.

MARGOT. Foxy.

GEORGE. Amy.

ALLAN. Those two don't get a vote.

ANN. Why not? That's democracy.

SAM. Even idiots get to vote.

ALFIE (*mutters*). Unfortunately.

GEORGE. Amy next.

ANTHEA. She's too ill.

MARGARET. She's still one of us.

ALLAN. Give her the watch then.

ANTHEA. She doesn't agree with it.

SAM. How do you know?

ALFIE. Yeah, let her speak for herself.

ANTHEA. She can't, can she.

MARGOT. She can whisper.

ANTHEA. She won't do it. She isn't evil like you.

ALLAN. Who's evil? This is fair.

ANN. This is democracy.

ENID. Yeah.

GEORGE. Give it to her.

ANTHEA *reluctantly passes* AMY *the watch.* AMY *holds it weakly.*

ANTHEA. See, she won't do it.

ENID. Give her a chance.

ANTHEA. She thinks it's wrong.

ALLAN. She hasn't said anything.

ENID. She wants to speak, look.

ANN. What's she saying?

ALLAN. Ssh!

ENID. Listen to her.

ANTHEA *leans down to listen to* AMY.

AMY. Foxy.

ANTHEA *looks shocked.*

ALLAN (*triumphant*). There you are.

ANTHEA. But Amy –

ALLAN. Told you.

ENID. She agrees with it.

ALLAN. Write that down.

GEORGE. I have.

MARGOT. You have to say why!

AMY. Because he's ginger.

ANTHEA. Can we stop this now?

MARGARET. Archie hasn't been.

MARGOT. Or Foxy.

ALFIE. Foxy doesn't get a vote.

GEORGE. If Amy gets one, Foxy should.

ANN. Yes that's only fair.

ALLAN. But he can't speak.

ENID. Maybe he'll finally bother.

ANN. I doubt it.

ENID. If his life's on the line.

SAM. We'll see about that.

ALFIE. Yeah, I wouldn't hold your breath.

ANN. Give him the watch.

ALLAN. But –

ANN. We must.

*They drag* FOXY *into the circle and hand him the watch. He just stares at them silently.*

ALLAN. Say your name and why you should get food.

ENID. Or water.

*Pause.*

ALLAN. See? Nothing.

ALFIE. Idiot.

ALLAN. Alright then. Nominate who you think shouldn't get any.

*Pause.*

ENID. I can't believe this.

ANN. Foxy?

ROGER. Foxy – if you were ever going to speak, then now is the time.

*Silence.*

ALLAN. Well that's a vote for himself.

ENID. Yeah, put down Foxy.

MARGARET. Foxy votes for Foxy!

SAM. Like a turkey voting for Christmas!

ALFIE. Idiot.

ENID. Who's next?

GEORGE. Just Archie.

ALLAN. Well go on then.

*They grab the watch from* FOXY *and hand it to* ARCHIE. *Pause while they all look at him.*

ARCHIE *is visibly trembling.*

ARCHIE. B – b – b – b – b –

ALFIE (*mocking*). B – b – b – b – !

SAM. Come on, you know how it works.

ENID. Say your name and why you should be saved.

ARCHIE. I – I – I – I – I –

ALFIE (*mocking*). You – you – you – you – you what?

ANTHEA. Stop it, let him speak.

ARCHIE. M – m – m – m – m –

ENID. This is ridiculous.

GEORGE. What's wrong with him?

SAM. Nominate someone then.

ALFIE. Yeah, nominate.

ENID. Or is that another vote for yourself?

ARCHIE. W – w – w – w – w –

ALFIE (*mocking*). W – w – w – w – w – WHAT?

SAM. Told you he was useless!

ALLAN. Come on, Archie, this is pathetic.

ANN. If there was ever a time to speak!

ALLAN. One last try!

ARCHIE. D – d – d – d – d – d – d –

ALFIE. D – d – d – die? Is that what you're trying to say?

SAM. Die! Haha! Die!

ENID. Die!

ANN. Die!

ALLAN. Die!

ALL. Die!

> ARCHIE *launches himself at* ALLAN *and stabs him once in the side with his penknife.*
>
> ALLAN *cries out and collapses.* ANN *goes to him.*
>
> *Others scream.*
>
> ALFIE *turns his loaded catapult on* ARCHIE.

ANN. You idiot!

ENID. What do you think you're doing?!

ALFIE. Back off!

> ARCHIE *backs away from* ALLAN *and* ANN *at the end of* ALFIE's *catapult.*
>
> *The others shrink and cower.*
>
> ENID *gathers the biscuits which have been knocked over.* ANN *inspects* ALLAN's *injury. It is bleeding.*

ANN. Oh God. Oh God, you're hurt.

ALLAN. It's fine.

*ALLAN's voice is trembling. He is in pain but trying not to show it.*

ANN. It's bleeding.

ALLAN. It's just a scratch.

ANN. No it isn't.

ALLAN. Please – just –

ANN. It's thick, and dark, and – oh God. Here, push here.

*ANN takes ALLAN's hand and presses it tight to his wound. Blood seeps through his fingers.*

Good. Don't move.

(*To* ALFIE, *of* ARCHIE.) Kill him.

ALLAN. No!

ANN. Do it.

ALLAN. No.

ANN. Shoot!

ALLAN. Don't.

*ALFIE hesitates, torn between ALLAN and ANN.*

ANN (*to* ALLAN). Why not?

ALLAN. Alfie and Archie have – have proved their worth.

ENID. What?

ALLAN. Bravery. Strength. Courage. It's what we need. Enid too. Bring them here.

ANN (*to* ALFIE, ARCHIE *and* ENID). Come closer.

ARCHIE. Wh-what?

ALFIE. Why?

ENID. You heard Allan. Come to this end.

*ARCHIE and ALFIE warily join ALLAN, ANN and ENID at one end of the boat. It is the end with the food and water.*

ALFIE *turns his loaded catapult away from* ARCHIE *and towards the rest of the group at the other end of the boat. They shrink and whimper as it is aimed at them.*

ALLAN (*weakly*). Get the book.

ANN *prods* ARCHIE *into action.* ARCHIE *goes to* GEORGE, *grabs his notebook and returns to the far end of the boat.* ALFIE *covers him the whole time with the catapult.*

Give it to me.

ALLAN *opens the book and prods a page, showing* ANN *his calculations.*

There's food and water, for six people, for two more days. There's five of us. Room for one more. Anthea.

ANN *nods and stands.*

ANN. Anthea. You may join us.

ANTHEA. But I'm – they need me. Amy needs me. And Roger, he –

ANN. Allan needs you.

ANTHEA. But –

ANN. They're not as important.

ANTHEA. I'm all they've got.

ANN. Allan's our leader.

ALLAN *is bleeding badly. He groans in pain.*

Come with us. There's room. You'll have biscuits. And water.

SAM. What about us?

ENID. There isn't room for any more.

ANTHEA. I'll care for all three.

ANN. No.

ANTHEA. Them and Allan.

ANN. No.

ANTHEA. Why not?

ANN. Because we need you.

ANTHEA. So do they.

ANN. They're finished.

ANTHEA. No.

ANN. Allan's strong. Come with us. Save yourself.

ANTHEA. Take Amy instead.

ENID. She's no use.

ANTHEA. She's more needy.

ENID. She's a burden.

ANN. Enid's right.

ANTHEA. Why can't I do both?

ANN. That's the deal, Anthea. Food, water, work. For us.

MARGARET. Anthea, no.

MARGOT. Don't do it.

GEORGE. Stay with us.

SAM. We need you too.

ENID. Quiet!

*ANTHEA agonises. She cries out in frustration. Then she walk to ALLAN's end of the boat.*

*The others cry out 'No!'*

ANTHEA. I'm sorry.

*ARCHIE, ALFIE and ENID mutter 'Yes', 'Well done', 'Good girl' – patting ANTHEA on the back.*

*ANTHEA inspects ALLAN's wound while trying not to cry.*

Bandages. And water. Just a little.

ENID. It's alright. We have enough now.

ANN. Alright, listen up. At this end, this is The Saved. At that end, is The Cursed. No longer are we thirteen, but six and seven. Separate. Free at last.

ANN *lays an oar down halfway.* ALFIE *and* ARCHIE *stand guard.*

No one shall cross this line. Or else.

GEORGE. Oh please.

SAM. No!

ROGER. You can't abandon us.

MARGOT. We don't want to be cursed!

MARGARET. What will we eat?

MARGOT. What will we drink?

SAM. This is murder!

GEORGE. Yeah!

ROGER. Scumbags…

SAM. We'll fight – won't we?

GEORGE. Yeah!

ROGER / MARGOT / MARGARET. Yeah!

SAM. We'll fight you!

GEORGE. We'll fight!

ALFIE *raises his catapult. They cower.*

ALFIE. Archie!

ARCHIE *draws his penknife and joins* ALFIE, *doing his best to look threatening. The other half of the group back down.*

MARGOT. Maybe we should pray instead?

MARGARET. Yes.

GEORGE. Yes, let's pray.

MARGOT *kneels. The others follow.*

MARGOT.
Our Father, who art in Heaven –

*The others join in.* ANTHEA *tends to* ALLAN.

ALFIE *keeps his catapult trained on the far end of the boat.*
ENID *repackages the biscuits.*

MARGOT / MARGARET / GEORGE / ROGER / SAM.
– hallowed be Thy name
Thy kingdom come
Thy will be done
On earth as it is in Heaven
Give us this day our daily bread
And forgive us our trespasses
As we forgive those who trespass against us
Lead us not into temptation
And deliver us from evil
For Thine is the kingdom
The power and the glory
Forever and ever
Amen

*Fog descends.*

### Day Four

*The fog clears on a desperate scene. Two camps, one at either end of the boat.*

*At one end:*

SAM *and* GEORGE *drum an empty tin can on the prow, repetitive, listless.* MARGARET *obsessively brushes her own hair, to the point where clumps are coming out.*

ROGER, *lying down, head bandaged, weakly holds up his watch to the sun in a vain attempt to navigate.*

MARGOT *tends to a shivering* AMY, *while clinging to her own doll Lilly.* FOXY *huddles somewhere among them.*

*At the other:*

ENID *traces a chalk circle round the end of the boat containing 'The Saved', drawing with extra force the new line across the middle of the boat.*

ANTHEA *mops* ALLAN's *brow; he is feverish. She is watched over by* ANN, *who occasionally interferes.*

ALFIE *and* ARCHIE *stand over an empty tin can in which pages from* GEORGE's *notebook are burning.* ARCHIE *tears out and hands more pages to* ALFIE. *They warm their hands.*

MARGOT. Oh no. Oh no.

MARGARET. What is it?

MARGOT *cradles her dolly.*

MARGOT. It's Lilly, she's, she's…

MARGARET. Oh no.

MARGOT. Poor Lilly.

MARGOT *crosses herself and crosses the dolly.*

MARGARET. We must give her a funeral.

MARGOT. Yes.

MARGARET. A Christian funeral.

MARGOT. Catholic.

MARGARET. A funeral at sea.

MARGOT. We need a coffin.

*The girls search around for one and take an old tin from the boys drumming. They solemnly place Lilly inside. They conduct a mini-funeral in the background while* ALLAN *and* ANN *talk* (*below*), *humming a hymn, with* MARGOT *presiding over proceedings. Even the boys get caught up, removing their hats and bowing their heads as the coffin passes by.*

ENID, *however, reinforces the chalk line in the middle of the boat and prevents the funeral coming to their end of the boat.*

*While* ANTHEA *watches the funeral,* ALLAN *and* ANN *talk.*

ALLAN. I had a dream last night.

ANN. Ssh, no need to talk.

ALLAN. But I want to tell you.

ANN. You're feverish.

ALLAN. We were on your uncle's lake. The one with the black swans.

ANN. My uncle's dead, Allan.

ALLAN. I was rowing. You were smiling. Your uncle was on the shore, waving.

ANN. He always did that.

ALLAN. It was hot.

ANN. How did you know he did that?

ALLAN. It was summer. The grass as dry as dust. The oak trees. The lake. Our boat. The sandstone house and the gravel drive.

ANN. Yes…

ALLAN. I rowed to the water's edge, stepped ashore, knelt before your uncle, and asked him.

ANN. Asked him?

ALLAN. For you. For your hand in marriage.

ANN. Oh, Allan.

ALLAN. He agreed.

ANN. Stop.

ALLAN. He agreed, Ann. And at that exact same moment all the swans on the lake, the jet-black swans, took off in flight and soared through the trees and into the sky, blocking out the sun.

ANN. Black as night.

ALLAN. Heavy as stormclouds.

ANN. Beautiful.

ALLAN. Frightening

ANN. But beautiful.

ALLAN. Yes.

ANN. You're breaking my heart. My uncle died next to that lake, defending his house.

ALLAN. Then it's a sign. From wherever he is. From the other side. We can get married, Ann. Your uncle said yes.

*She touches his forehead and face.*

ANN. You're burning up. (*To* ANTHEA.) Water.

*ANN gestures to ANTHEA, who breaks away from watching Lilly's funeral and goes to fetch some.*

*At the other end of the boat, Lilly in her coffin has reached the edge of the boat and* MARGOT *is saying a final psalm.*

MARGOT. 'I am the resurrection and the life. He who believes in me will live, even though he dies.'

*The others murmur 'Amen'.*

MARGOT *lets the tin coffin fall into the water with a splash. She turns and cries on* MARGARET's *shoulder.*

MARGARET. 'Blessed are those who mourn, for they will be comforted.'

ANTHEA *finds that the open water tin they have been drinking from is empty and she finds she needs to open another. She approaches* ANN.

ANTHEA. I need the tin opener. For the final water. I'm sorry.

ANN *reaches for it in her pocket but it isn't there. She pats herself down then looks on the floor.*

ANN. Where's the tin opener?

ANTHEA. I don't know.

ANN. Who's got it?

ENID. Not me.

ANN. Look for it!

ARCHIE. Look for w-what?

ANN. The tin opener. It's gone.

ALFIE. It can't have.

ANTHEA. You had it.

ENID. Help us look.

ALFIE. Where did you leave it?

ANN. Nowhere.

ANTHEA. It must be somewhere.

ANN. Well it isn't.

ARCHIE. Maybe you d-dropped it.

ANN. Of course I didn't. Someone's stolen it!

ANTHEA. You mean a thief?

ALFIE. A traitor.

ENID. A Judas!

ANN. There's a traitor on the boat!

ENID. Own up! Who was it?

*They turn on the others at the other end.*

*A chorus of 'Not me!', 'I haven't seen it!', 'Who would do that?', 'I don't know what you're talking about!'*

ANN. Whoever has done this deserves to die! You've killed us all.

*Whimpering.*

ALFIE. We'll break them open!

ARCHIE. Yeah!

ALFIE. We're strong enough!

ALFIE *and* ARCHIE *try to break into the last water tin by smashing it.*

ANN. Stop it!

ROGER (*weakly*). Maybe… The Saved aren't so saved after all.

ANN. What was that?

ROGER. Maybe… we're all in this together. Maybe we always were.

ANN. That's a disgusting thing to say.

ENID. Have you got it then?

ALFIE. Yeah are you the thief?

ARCHIE. You b-betrayed us.

ALFIE. Yeah, protected Foxy.

ENID. Someone useless.

ANN. And you paid the price.

ALFIE. Yeah.

ANN. Is this your revenge?

ROGER. No.

*ARCHIE and ALFIE draw their weapons.*

ANN. Prove it.

ROGER. What?

ANN. Prove it.

ROGER. How?

ANN. Frisk him.

ALFIE. Yeah we'll find it.

ENID. He'll have it on him.

ARCHIE. Roger's the th-thief.

*ALFIE and ARCHIE roughly frisk ROGER but don't find the tin opener. However they do find half a chocolate bar.*

ALFIE. What's this?

ARCHIE. Ch-chocolate?

ANN. Chocolate?

MARGOT. Chocolate!

SAM. Let's see!

ALFIE. Half a bar.

ANN. And you kept this secret?

GEORGE. Let's have some.

ARCHIE. It's m-mine.

ALFIE. I found it.

ENID. Give it here.

ANN (*with authority*). I'll take it.

> *Pause.* ANN *examines it. She takes a piece and bites it in half. She feeds the other half to* ALLAN.

'All in this together.' You snake.

ROGER. I was saving it.

ENID. What for?

ROGER. For our rescue.

ALFIE. Why?

ROGER. To celebrate.

ENID. Liar. You were saving it for yourself.

ANN. Well now it belongs to us. Me and Allan.

ANTHEA. Can I have some?

ANN. No.

ENID. Oh, this is our curse! I thought we were rid of it but look! We're thirteen – still.

ANN. Enid's right.

GEORGE. I thought we were six and seven?

ANN. You can't fool nature. Any time there is thirteen people, the door is open for evil.

ROGER. That's ridiculous.

ENID. What more proof do you need? This is our fourth day without rescue.

ANN. She's right.

ENID. First we were thirteen – too many for the rations we had.

ANN. Then there was Allan's scarf – our flag – lost, in the dead of night.

ENID. Then Allan himself – our leader – mortally wounded.

ANN. And now this. The tin opener. Lost – stolen – whatever. But without it we're dead.

ENID. We're out of warnings. Next will come the storm.

ANN. That's right. So long as we are thirteen, our luck will not change.

*Whimpering.*

ALLAN. Unless we break it.

ANN. Unless we break it.

ALLAN. But how?

ALFIE. I can think of a way.

*ALFIE and ARCHIE face the far end of the boat with their weapons.*

ARCHIE. Yeah, who's it g-going to be?

*The others cower.*

ANN. We need a ceremony.

ENID. What?

ANN. A ritual. To break the curse. To save us all.

ANTHEA. You mean like a ceremony?

ENID. She just said that, idiot.

MARGOT. An exorcism.

ANN. Something for good luck. To lift our spirits. To fill us with glory. To prove that we're going to live.

ALFIE. Like what?

*ANN laughs, then claps her hands*

ANN. Allan has proposed to me. And I've decided to accept.

ALLAN. Oh, Ann…

ANN. We're going to get married. There's going to be a wedding.

ANN *kisses* ALLAN.

*The others stop and stare.*

*Then murmuring, becoming more excitable, rising to a crescendo of cries and claps.*

MARGARET. What – on the boat?

ENID. Yes!

MARGARET. A wedding?

MARGOT. A wedding!

GEORGE. There's going to be a wedding.

SAM. To break the curse.

ANTHEA. To lift our spirits.

ENID. To fill us with glory.

MARGARET. There's a pair of lovers on the boat!

MARGOT. Allan and Ann are in love!

SAM. And they're going to get married.

GEORGE. To save us all.

ENID. To banish evil.

MARGOT. We're saved.

MARGARET. We're saved.

ALL. We're saved!

SAM (*taking* MARGOT*'s hand*). We're going to get married too!

GEORGE (*taking* MARGARET*'s hand*). And us!

ALFIE (*taking* ANTHEA*'s hand*). And us!

ANTHEA. Eurgh, no we're not!

ANN (*firmly*). NO.

*Pause.*

MARGOT. Why not?

ANN. There isn't room for more than one couple.

MARGARET. Why not?

ANN. There isn't enough food.

SAM. There isn't any food.

ALLAN. We must write it down. To make it official.

*ALLAN winces as he moves.*

ANN. Darling, careful.

ALLAN. Everyone must sign their names. To show this isn't just a dream.

*ALFIE tears a page out of GEORGE's pad and hands it to ALLAN with the pencil. ALLAN writes the hands the paper round, everyone signs.*

GEORGE. But all weddings have food.

SAM. That's right, they have feasts. I've been to one.

ARCHIE. So have I. It was b-brilliant.

ALFIE. Where's our feast going to come from?

ANN. It's going to be the best feast you've ever seen. More food than you could ever imagine.

ALFIE. How?

GEORGE. Will there be a roast?

ANN. Yes. A whole hog roast, with all the trimmings.

GEORGE. Mmmm

SAM. Like crunchy potatoes?

ANN. And parsnips.

MARGARET. And buttered carrots?

MARGOT. What about leeks?

ANN. Definitely. And bread sauce, and cranberry –

ANTHEA. Like Christmas!

ANN. Litres of lemonade –

GEORGE. And onion gravy!

SAM. Delicious!

MARGARET. Oh I want it!

ANN. Then sticky toffee pudding –

MARGARET. I want it now!

MARGOT. Custard –

ENID. Cream –

ANTHEA. Sherry trifle –

ALFIE. And cheese!

SAM. Cheese!

ALL. Cheeeeeeeese!

*They lick and chew the air manically, as if they can taste these things.* ANN *and* ALLAN *kiss again.*

ALFIE *takes the paper that* ALLAN *has been writing on and waves it.*

ALFIE. Let the world bear witness!

ENID. A declaration of love!

ANN. Forever!

GEORGE. Can I have my pad?

ALFIE (*threateningly*). Stay on your side.

GEORGE. I thought we weren't cursed any more.

ALFIE. Not yet you're not.

ARCHIE. Not till after the w-wedding.

*The signed paper has made its way back round to* ALLAN.

ALLAN (*to* ANN). Your Thermos.

ANN. What?

ALLAN. To put it in.

ANN. Oh.

ALLAN. Every message needs a bottle.

> ANN *fetches her Thermos and hands it to* ALLAN.
>
> ALLAN *receives the paper back. He reads the list of signatures.*

ROGER (*weakly*). And Foxy.

ANN. What?

ROGER. Foxy too. He mustn't be left out.

MARGARET. But he can't even write.

ENID. Or talk.

MARGOT. He doesn't do anything.

SAM. Or say anything.

ALFIE. He doesn't matter.

ANN. Yes, he isn't even real.

> ALLAN *folds the message and places it inside the Thermos and seals it. He tries to stand but the pain is too much.*

Careful!

ENID. You can't.

ANN. Sit down.

> ALLAN *hands the Thermos to* ALFIE.

ALLAN. You do it. Let the world hear the news! Allan and Ann are one in life and in death!

ALL. Hooray!

> ALFIE *flings the Thermos far out to sea, where it lands with a distant splash.* ALLAN *pulls* ANN *close and whispers in her ear.* (*See postscript on p. 127.*)

MARGARET. It floats!

GEORGE. Of course it floats, that's physics.

ARCHIE. That will n-never sink.

ALFIE. Red too – that can easily be seen.

MARGOT. Easily.

ANN. Now we must prepare.

GEORGE. How?

ANN. It must go just like a real wedding – all the rituals – for good luck.

ANTHEA. Something old.

MARGOT. Something new.

MARGARET. Something borrowed.

ENID. Something blue.

ANN. To break the curse. Our curse. Forever.

ENID. Yes.

ANTHEA. Anything.

MARGARET. Everything.

MARGOT. Tell us.

GEORGE. It's your day.

ALFIE. Just tell us what you want.

ANN. Tomorrow – here's how it's going to go…

*ANN beckons them into a huddle and whispers. The fog envelops them and they are lost from view.*

## Day Five

*A hive of activity on board the boat as everyone prepares for the wedding. The divide into two groups has been forgotten and everyone moves freely from one end to the other.*

*The three bridesmaids* (MARGARET, MARGOT *and* ENID) *fuss around* ANN, *arranging her hair and adding or removing various items of clothing and other trinkets, such as bracelets, which they were previously wearing themselves. They end by tying the spare sail around her neck and trailing it behind her like a long bridal train, each taking a corner.*

ANTHEA *has arranged the three invalids* – AMY, ROGER *and* ALLAN – *sat up in a line. She fusses around each of them in turn, mopping their brows and checking their dressings. Every now and then she ducks out of sight behind the sail to the 'kitchen' to prepare the 'feast' – the remaining biscuits in piles.*

*As best man,* ROGER *consults seriously with* ALLAN *in a whisper, showing him a selection of rings he has gathered from the girls, for* ALLAN *to choose one as their wedding ring.*

*As priest,* GEORGE *has made himself a makeshift cassock from the canvas bag that contained the tins. He is busy lashing two of his pencils together into a crucifix using string.*

ARCHIE *and* ALFIE *stand guard over everyone, solemnly.* FOXY *is nowhere to be seen, but rustling occasionally comes from the kitchen area when* ANTHEA *is not in it.*

*A storm rumbles in the distance. It becomes closer throughout this scene.* ANN *raises one hand and everyone stops what they are doing.*

GEORGE. It's time! It's time!

ANN. We must hurry. We don't have long. The storm is coming.

*The children arrange themselves into two rows.* GEORGE *makes sure they are symmetrical on either side of the boat.*

GEORGE. Stand up straight. Ready?

GEORGE *mimes pulling a bell chord and the children burst out with 'Ding dong! Ding dong!', imitating church bells.*

ANN. Who's going to give me away?

ALFIE. Me!

ENID. How old-fashioned.

MARGOT. You're not her dad.

ALFIE. I'm her guardian.

> ANN *takes* ALFIE's *arm and walks with him to the 'church' where* GEORGE *as priest is waiting, holding his crucifix pencils, with* ALLAN *and best man* ROGER. *The bridesmaids walk behind them, carrying* ANN's *train.*
>
> *Perhaps the others hum a hymn – 'Amazing Grace', if so.*
>
> GEORGE *arranges everyone into rows on the church pews.* ALLAN *and* ANN *are directed to the 'altar', a pile of empty tin cans.*

ANN (*to* ALLAN). Now the priest appears, that's George. He'll do the ceremony. You have been to a wedding, haven't you?

ALLAN. I didn't pay much attention.

> GEORGE *stands before them holding his crucifix.*

ANN (*to* GEORGE). You have, haven't you?

GEORGE. Lots.

ANN. Good. (*To* ALLAN.) Just watch us. (*To* GEORGE.) It's alright if you can't remember it all, the service for children is shorter than for adults.

GEORGE. Alright. (*To congregation.*) You may sit.

> *They sit.*

We are gathered here today to bear witness to the marriage of Allan and Ann, and to give thanks for their union before Almighty God.

CONGREGATION. Amen.

GEORGE. Wait till the end to say that.

CONGREGATION. Sorry.

GEORGE. Now then. Does anyone know any objections why these two cannot be joined in holy matrimony? Speak now or forever hold your peace.

*Silence, save for the approaching storm.*

Then we shall proceed.

ROGER *steps up with the ring. He is unsteady on his feet.*

Do you, Ann, take this boy, Allan, to be your lawful wedded husband, to have and to hold, in sickness and health, forever and ever so help you God amen?

ANN. I do.

GEORGE. And do you, Allan, take this girl, Ann, to be your lawful wedded wife?

ALLAN. I do.

GEORGE. Best man.

GEORGE *takes the ring from* ROGER *and hands it to* ALLAN, *who puts it on* ANN*'s ring finger.*

I now declare you husband and wife! You may kiss the bride.

ALLAN *kisses* ANN *coyly.*

Hip-hip!

ALL. Hooray!

GEORGE. Hip-hip!

ALL. Hooray!

GEORGE. Hip-hip!

ALL. Hooray!

GEORGE *scatters torn up notebook pages as confetti as everyone cheers and applauds.*

ALLAN. Are we – ?

ANN. We're still in church. Another hymn!

*The children sing 'Jerusalem' as* ALLAN, ANN *and bridesmaids walk solemnly to the other end of the boat.*

*In the sea, through the fog, black swans glide into view, their necks long and twisted.*

Look – Allan – our swans!

ALLAN. Oh! Oh, Ann…

ALLAN *and* ANN *watch as their swans swish around them in the mist. The other children continue to sing 'Jerusalem', softly, unaware of the swans. Thunder rumbles, and rain begins to fall.*

*All of a sudden the swans take off, the noise of their wings filling the air and momentarily obscuring the sun.*

Terrifying.

ANN. Beautiful!

ANN *raises her hand – the other children stop singing. The storm and the rain continues around them.*

Time for the feast!

SAM. Yes!

ANN. Call forth the cook!

ALL. The cook! The cook!

ANTHEA. I'm here!

ANN. What are you doing there? (*i.e. tending to* AMY *and* ROGER *rather than in the kitchen area.*)

ALLAN. Where's the food?

ANTHEA. It's all prepared.

ALFIE. Why aren't you looking after it?

ANTHEA. I was looking after my patients too.

ARCHIE. Food is p-precious.

ANTHEA. I'm not a guard – you are.

ROGER. It's alright, there's enough to go around.

ALFIE. If only.

ALLAN. Bring on the feast.

ALL. The feast! The feast!

ANTHEA *goes to the makeshift tent at the end of the boat and pulls back the sail theatrically, as if to reveal the feast.*

*But behind the sail is* FOXY, *sitting on his own, surrounded by empty tins and biscuit crumbs, crumbs all down his front, a half-eaten biscuit in each hand and a full mouth, crumbs spilling out.*

*Everyone gasps.*

ANN. No!

ALLAN. Foxy!

ANN. No!

ENID. He's eating it!

SAM. He's eaten it!

GEORGE. All of it!

MARGARET. The feast!

MARGOT. Our feast!

AMY. Stop him!

ALLAN. He's wasting it!

ANN. Ruined!

ARCHIE. Oh G-God!

ROGER. Foxy!

SAM. Crumbs… nothing but crumbs.

ENID. Greedy –

MARGOT. Little –

ALL. PIG!

ANN (*to* ANTHEA). What were you thinking?

ANTHEA. I'm sorry!

ALFIE. Did you know?

ANTHEA. Of course not!

ENID. You let him!

ANTHEA. No!

ARCHIE. You were the ch-chef!

ANTHEA. I was looking after my patients too!

SAM. Stupid –

GEORGE. Stupid –

ALFIE. Traitor!

ANTHEA. It's not my fault!

ALLAN. Of course it is!

ANTHEA. It's not – it's Foxy's!

MARGARET. Foxy –

MARGOT. Foxy –

ROGER. No!

ANN. Foxy has killed us all!

ALLAN. And ruined our wedding!

SAM. Nothing – nothing left!

ROGER. Wait, he's small –

GEORGE. Parasite!

ROGER. He was hungry –

ENID. Vermin!

ROGER. You starved him!

ALFIE. Scum!

ANN. We're all starving!

ALLAN. But he's eaten it.

MARGARET. Everything –

MARGOT. Everything!

AMY. He must pay.

ANN. Yes.

ALLAN. Yes.

ALL. Yes!

ROGER. No!

*ENID starts chanting.*

ENID.
Teddy Bear, Teddy Bear –

MARGOT *joins in*

ENID / MARGOT.
Turn around.
Teddy Bear, Teddy Bear –

*Others join in until everyone but ROGER is chanting.*

ALL (*except* ROGER).
Touch the ground.
Teddy Bear, Teddy Bear,
Touch your shoe.
Teddy Bear, Teddy Bear,
That will do.

ROGER *scrambles to place himself between the rest of the group and* FOXY *as they advance on him.*

ROGER. No – no.

ALL (*except* ROGER).
Teddy Bear, Teddy Bear,
Go upstairs.
Teddy Bear, Teddy Bear,
Say your prayers.

ROGER. Please. Please.

ALFIE *and* ARCHIE *draw their weapons and turn them on* ROGER, *who is now all that stands between the group and* FOXY, *who is now pinned up against the far prow.*

ALL (*except* ROGER).
Teddy Bear, Teddy Bear,
Turn out the light.

Teddy Bear, Teddy Bear
Say goodnight!

*The storm hits with full force – crashing thunder, and dark, heavy rain.* ROGER *screams.*

*Darkness descends as stormclouds envelop the boat. Drumming.*

*A splash as a body falls into water.*

**Day Six**

*The fog lies heavily on the sea, blotting out the boat. A soft breeze thins the mist slowly, until the last strands have lifted from the boat. Bright sunlight.*

*Between the seats, the children slump, listless, silent and drenched from the storm.* FOXY *is no longer among them.*

*The distant whump-whump of a helicopter, high up in the air. It gets closer.*

SAM. A plane… a plane!

*Gradually the other children straighten up and come round.* ROGER *is the only one who doesn't get excited.*

GEORGE. A plane!

ALFIE. A plane!

ARCHIE. Where?

MARGOT. I can't see it.

SAM. Up there!

ALFIE. That's a helicopter.

MARGARET. Where?

ENID. There's still fog.

GEORGE. It's clearing – see the blue.

ANTHEA. There – there!

ENID. I see it!

MARGOT. A plane!

GEORGE. A helicopter!

SAM. A helicopter!

*Chorus of: 'A helicopter!', 'Thank God', 'We're saved!' Then a clamour of shouting and waving to attract its attention: 'Over here!', 'We're here!', 'Down here!', 'This way!', 'Please – please!'*

*ANN crawls out from under the spare sail that she used yesterday as a wedding dress. ALLAN is also under there.*

MARGARET. Ann – a plane!

ALFIE. A helicopter!

ENID. Over there!

ANTHEA. Please don't fly past – please!

*ANN claps her hands over her mouth. She is emotional.*

ANN. It worked. We're saved. Oh God. Oh God.

*The children fall silent, then whisper guiltily:*

ALL. It worked. We're saved.

*ALLAN comes out from under the sail tent.*

ALLAN. What worked?

SAM. We're rescued.

ANN. There's a helicopter.

ALLAN. Oh… oh! Here! Over here!

*ALLAN starts to wave but ANN suddenly rushes to him and flings her arms around him. ANN sobs, unnerving ALLAN.*

SAM. It's circling!

ALFIE. It's stopping!

ARCHIE. It's seen us!

SAM. I heard it first – me!

ALLAN (*to* ANN). Don't. Don't. Stop it.

*ALLAN struggles with* ANN, *both are distraught,* ALLAN *trying to hide it.* ROGER *stares at them witheringly.*

ARCHIE. They're descending.

ALFIE. Getting closer.

MARGOT. They've seen us!

MARGARET. We're saved!

ALLAN *pushes* ANN *away.*

ANN. You did this!

ALLAN. We did this! Us! Leaders.

ROGER. You all did it.

ALLAN. You're lucky we didn't do you as well.

*The children fall silent.*

He sacrificed himself – for us. He did the bravest, noblest, kindest thing –

ROGER. You can't even say his name.

*Pause.*

ALLAN (*defiantly*). Foxy.

ANTHEA. You made us hate him.

ALLAN. You hated him already. He was killing us all with his laziness and greed.

ROGER. It was wrong.

ALLAN. This was a war.

ANTHEA *cries.*

*The helicopter noise gets closer.*

But we won. We broke the curse. And now we're all free.

ANTHEA. I'm going to tell them.

ALFIE. No!

ARCHIE. No!

ENID. No!

ALLAN. We must never speak of this. Never.

ENID. How many are we?

ALFIE. Twelve.

MARGOT. Twelve.

SAM. Twelve.

ALLAN. And we always were.

ROGER. Like the disciples?

ALLAN. Like children. Innocents. The rest went down with the ship.

*Pause.*

Understood?

*Nodding and murmuring.*

(*Louder.*) Understood?

ALL. Yes, Allan.

ALFIE. We must dispose of everything.

SAM. Everything?

ALFIE. Everything.

*ALFIE starts with his catapult, which he throws overboard. ARCHIE throws his penknife.*

*Everyone throws something overboard: MARGARET her hairbrush, GEORGE his pencils and the remainder of his pad, SAM his marbles, ENID her chalk, MARGOT the remaining tins, ANTHEA the bloody bandages.*

*ANN takes out Foxy's torch. She looks at it. She is suddenly wracked with trembling sobs.*

*The helicopter is now directly overhead, blasting their clothes, hair and whipping up the water. A spotlight swings back and forth, illuminating the boat in waves of white light.*

*A rope ladder clatters down. One by one they climb up, with* ROGER *and* ANTHEA *helping* AMY, *until only* ALLAN *and* ANN *are left.* ALLAN *tugs at* ANN *but she refuses to climb.*

*He kisses her; she pushes him away. He says something; we can't hear what.*

*He screams at her; she shakes her head and continues to cradle Foxy's torch.*

ALLAN *takes something out of his pocket – the tin opener. He pushes it into her hands, then backs away.*

ANN *screams and sobs.*

ALLAN *climbs up the rope ladder.*

ANN *flings the torch and the tin opener overboard.*

*The rope ladder hovers; she grabs it and flings it with all her might. It swings back and forth across the deck.*

*Slowly, it begins to rise up.*

ANN *collapses to the deck. Fog descends.*

*The sound of the helicopter moving away.*

## Epilogue

*Darkness.*

*The sound of the sea. Distantly, the sound of a war. The sound of the wind.*

*The sound of the sea. Darkness.*

## Postscript

When Allan whispers in Ann's ear on p. 113, here is what he says:

ALLAN. That – (*The message in the Thermos.*) won't work unless we make it.

ANN. How do you mean?

ALLAN. I've worked out how to save us, but I need you to do everything I say.

ANN. Alright.

ALLAN. Prepare for the wedding. It must go just like a real wedding – all the rituals – for good luck. Give everyone a job. Leave the rest to me.

ANN. What are you planning?

ALLAN. Just trust me. I'm going to break our curse.

# LIFE RAFT:
# THE GAMES

*Tassos Stevens
and Fin Kennedy*

## TASSOS STEVENS

Tassos Stevens is a playmaker – of (at time of writing) twenty-seven years' professional and fifty years' personal experience – making all kinds of play and games to spark change.

The only other important stuff to share here: he was the lead/co-founder of Coney, an award-winning arts and social-change charity, but most – no, actually none :) – of the brilliant stuff in its lifetime happened without other brilliant people: including here, in this playmaking approach of games to accompany *Life Raft*, David Finnigan and Melanie Frances, both brilliant associates of Coney.

Tassos will found a future venture, operating locally and everywhere, starting in Gloucester where he lives currently. If you ever want a helping hand with these games, feel free to drop a line to: theplayfuldoc@gmail.com.

**Playing Games**

This section of the book is about making (and playing) games located in the world, and within the events and themes, of Fin Kennedy's play *Life Raft*.

Reading it could simply enrich your understanding of what happens in the play, and also offer jumping-off points for further exploration.

Or it could help you – and a group – into a richer rehearsal process if you're staging your own production of the play.

Or you and a group together could take what's here to build your own performance game (or games!) based on the world of *Life Raft*, adapting it to suit your participants. This may have the added bonus of fully involving and engaging a group, because the process of making games is essentially democratic and, as games are themselves best made through playing them, can be very fun indeed.

Or perhaps all of the above!

\*

Let's begin with a couple of definitions of 'game', because you're quite possibly thinking about video games when you read the word, and that's not what we're talking about here.

A game can be defined as a combination of:

- A playing objective – for instance, what you need to do to win.
- An obstacle – which makes the achieving of that objective more challenging or interesting.
- Feedback – which lets you know how well you're doing.

So in the simple game of *Keepy-Uppy*, for instance, the playing objective is to keep hitting the ball up in the air; the obstacle is gravity; and the feedback is your running count of how many times you've kept it up.

This definition is useful here because the framework of playing objectives – and obstacles – intersects with the preparation that an actor might make towards playing a scene.

A game can also be defined as a system you can play: a way of simulating a situation, understanding what's in play, and exploring more possibilities of what could happen.

In the world of *Life Raft*, we have a situation where a group of young people are on a raft in the middle of an ocean, with limited supplies and no way of knowing when – or if – they might be rescued. We have all the interpersonal interplays between the different young people that make up this group. And we have external events, good or bad, that could happen to influence their fate, such as storms.

We're going to give you some building blocks of gameplay based on each of these – limited supplies; events and fate; interpersonal interplay – which you and a group can use to make your game.

Note that once we've introduced the basics, the instructions become more 'open'. That's deliberate – to allow you and your group to riff on these elements, to build your own version of the game, and ultimately your own story.

But first of all, let's explain how to make games through playing games.

**The Game's Afoot**

This is a game that wraps around another game, playing and changing it to make it more fun. This is essentially how we make games. *The Game's Afoot* can be wrapped around any simple game that the whole group can play, ideally one that is quick to play and easily replayable. A simple game we'd recommend is *Grandmother's Footsteps*:

*Grandmother's Footsteps*

This game is closely related to others like *Red Light Green Light* and *What's the Time, Mr Wolf?* It's typically played with eight to fifteen players, but you can easily play with more or fewer.

- One player is Grandma, who stands at one end of the playspace with their back to the room.
- A distance away, behind the starting line, everyone else plays the Grandkids.
- The objective for the Grandkids is to be the first to tap Grandma on the shoulder – they then win and will become Grandma the next time you play.
- The obstacle, as well as the other Grandkids, is that every so often, without warning, Grandma will turn around and then the Grandkids must freeze, motionless. If Grandma spots anyone moving, those Grandkids are sent back to the starting line.
- Grandma then turns her back on the Grandkids, until the next time she chooses to turn around again, the Grandkids freeze… and repeat until one of the Grandkids taps her on the shoulder. They win, and will become Grandma the next time you play.

And that's it, hopefully over in a couple of minutes tops. Play this first of all, and then move into *The Game's Afoot*.

*The Game's Afoot: A Game-Making Process*

Ask everyone to answer: 'Was that fun for you?' Thumbs up for fun, thumbs down for not fun, thumbs level for unsure. Encourage the group to be honest; you're expecting that some will find it more fun than others.

You can also ask: 'Which specific moments in play were the most fun for you? And what happened in those moments?' Again, be honest; everyone will have their own ideas of what was fun.

Now, you can introduce the objective of *The Game's Afoot*: to change the game you're playing, in order to make it as fun as possible for *everyone*. And you'll do that by asking one of the players to suggest one simple change or addition to the rules.

For example, the Grandkids have to hop on one leg. Or they have to sing when they're moving. Or Grandma has to count down from five and only turn when they get to zero. Or only gets to send three Grandkids back in total. (In one memorable addition during playtesting, Grandma shot Grandkids with a shotgun, who then had to perform an over-the-top stage death.)

Ideally, you'll say yes to the first suggestion for a rule-change without discussing if it's a good idea or a bad idea. Instead, you'll just start playing this new version of the game.

When you've finished playing a second time, you can now ask again for a show of thumbs. Thumbs up if that rule-change made it more fun to play. Thumbs down if it made it less fun. Thumbs level if it was about the same.

And you might again ask for moments that were most fun. Remember it's what is fun for everyone; not just different people but also the different roles: Grandma, the Grandkids, and indeed anyone watching as an audience.

And then another show of thumbs. Thumbs up to keep the rule-change, thumbs down to drop it.

Then, whether you kept that change or dropped it, ask for another suggestion for one simple change or addition to the rules that might make the game more fun for everyone to play.

And play *Grandmother's Footsteps* again. And judge how fun. And vote to keep or drop. And another suggestion. And repeat at least one more time, or until it stops being fun.

\*

This is a game-making process, playing one rule-change at a time. It's also a model of any iterative creative process. It's also an important mechanism within stories. Successive complications raise the stakes for the characters (as in *Life Raft*), which makes them more interesting to watch.

Instead of 'fun' you can substitute 'interesting', 'beautiful', 'meaningful' – indeed any word matching the value that is most important for you and the game – but fun is really important for games. They don't happen without it.

*Breaking Games*

Another way to make a new game is to break an old game, in a challenge we call *The Broken Game*. Take *Rock Paper Scissors*, which is a game for two players that we're sure you already know. Two players face off and on a count of three, they make a rock or scissors or paper with their hands to see who wins: rock blunts scissors, scissors cut paper, paper wraps rock.

You can break this game very simply by dividing everyone into groups of three, four or five, and then challenging them in a short amount of time to evolve a new game that works for that many people to play. Each group then demonstrates their new game, ideally teaching another group how to play it. And then everyone can vote for which of the new games is most fun.

**Playing *Life Raft***

The situation of the play *Life Raft*, with survivors adrift in the middle of an ocean, with no idea if or when a ship will appear to save them before they run out of food, is what drives the drama between characters.

First is a game based on this situation, which can act as an engine to generate similar drama: *The Biscuit Game*. If you have limited time, or only one session, play this first of all – to understand the gameplay – with small groups of players as survivors on a life raft, each facilitated by one player as an angel.

If you have longer, or several sessions, you might want to start with *Angel Academy*, in which trainee angels compete to make the most interesting story happen. That learning can then be applied in *The Biscuit Game*.

Finally, *A Life Well Played* can be wrapped around *The Biscuit Game* to develop individual characters and reflect on their playing experience afterwards.

Note that any game simulating *Life Raft* is a performance game, designed to make a performance happen. We want players not necessarily to win – or even survive – but rather play and perform their characters well.

We'd recommend you play *The Biscuit Game* and *Angel Academy* each separately with your group, then read on for notes on integrating them into a full performance game.

Taking these three games as building blocks, and with the tools to change games, you can make a rich performance game based on *Life Raft*, and ultimately perhaps, your own show.

## The Biscuit Game
*Designed by David Finnigan,
with development through playtesting by Melanie Frances,
Fin Kennedy and Tassos Stevens*

What follows is a combination of rules and a description of gameplay. We recommend that you read through this first of all by yourself – as well as assembling the props you will need. If practical, you might also want to appoint some angels ahead of time from among your group, and let them read these instructions in advance, too.

If you're working with an older group, you may want to read the instructions through with the whole group at the top of the session; if younger players, it might be better to jump straight in and let them pick it up. If possible, let your group drive.

### *The Gameplay*

This is a game of managing a limited supply of food – biscuits – between a number of survivors on board a life raft. If the group is not familiar with the play *Life Raft*, it will be helpful to read the opening pages aloud here to set the scene (pages 15–23, by which time all thirteen characters have spoken at least once).

*Survivors* need biscuits to stay alive, keeping track of their health via a traffic-light system, but they don't know when a ship might arrive to rescue them. The group may discuss how biscuits will be shared, but players may choose to steal or hoard biscuits, or give them to others. Maybe a survivor only cares for themselves, maybe they are looking out for all. This is a chance for individual actors to develop a character and play it.

*Angels* narrate and facilitate play, and may later introduce events to keep the story interesting.

*Players*

We'd recommend first of all playing *The Biscuit Game* with several small groups of five to seven players. We reckon it can easily be played with thirteen players to model the play's cast of characters, even as many as eighteen; but the more players, the more additional structure or facilitation support will be needed. Playing with smaller groups at first means that you and your group can grasp the basic dynamic of the game. Later you can add more players or other changes to make it more fun and/or interesting.

Divide the room into smaller groups of between five and seven players. Each group sits in a circle, making their life raft. Each group is playing their own game, independently from the other groups, although they should all be able to run simultaneously. Ideally most groups will have the same number of players, simply because that will give them the best chance of finishing at roughly the same time.

One player in each group should take the role of an *angel*, in order to facilitate their group's game. The others are playing people on board the life raft, we'll call them the *survivors*.

The basic game might take fifteen to twenty minutes to play.

*Props*

You'll need two cups or other containers for each group. Give these to each group's angel to begin with.

You'll need some dice, at least one per group. Also give these to the angel in the group.

You'll need a *lot* of counters of some kind to represent biscuits. You could use game counters, or dried beans, or jigsaw pieces. Whatever you use, we're going to call them *biscuits* from now on.

Each group receives three times the number of biscuits as survivors on their boat. So, a group of seven players would receive twenty-one biscuits, for example.

The biscuits are placed in one of the cups to begin with, for the angel to look after. Angels will need a copy of the daily scripts (the sections in *italics* below).

THE GAMES  139

*Health*

Every *survivor* should have a sheet of paper and a pen.

Ask them to write down with space in between:

      GREEN      AMBER      RED

on their sheet and keep that in front of them.

This is their health-o-meter. Green means they're in good health, red means they're in poor health, amber in between. If a survivor's health drops a level below red, then they're not a survivor. They're dead.

Each survivor in turn should roll a dice, to determine the health they start with:

- If they roll *4*, *5* or *6*: their health starts as *green*.
- If they roll *2* or *3*: their health starts as *amber*.
- If they roll *1*: their health starts as *red*.

Each survivor can use their pen to indicate their position on the health-o-meter.

Each day, the survivors' health is impacted by the biscuits they 'eat'.

- If they eat *two or more* biscuits, their health *rises one level*. It can't rise beyond green.
- If they eat *one* biscuit, their health *stays where it is*.
- If they eat *no* biscuits, their health *drops one level*.

If they drop below red, they're dead. There's a short punctuation while they leave the game, either to spectate or to join the ranks of the angels.

*The First Round of Play: Monday*

The angels control the clock, and announce the time at various intervals, so as to keep play moving.

The game starts, and the angel speaks, something along the lines of:

*It's a Monday morning, in the middle of the ocean.*

*You don't know how many days before a ship will appear to rescue you.*

*First of all, count your biscuits. Then discuss how many biscuits each person will receive today. You need to reach an agreement before the sun reaches noon.*

Perhaps each survivor might introduce themselves in turn, and say why they hope to survive.

(NB: If you are playing the game not for the first time, and are ready to develop more detailed characters – for example, having played *A Life Well Played* – then there is an opportunity at this point to add in some individual characterisation. Have a look at how the characters of *Life Raft* are described in the character list on page 13. After their name and age, each has three adjectives. You could ask survivors to do this for their own characters here, then try to play those characteristics during the game. But play once without this first, to grasp the game mechanics.)

Once everyone has discussed and agreed how to allocate biscuits, then the angel hands out the designated number of biscuits to each survivor.

Each survivor in turn then chooses how many biscuits to eat; any they don't eat are kept in their hand for the next day.

The 'eaten' biscuits are placed in the second cup, now out of play (it is the angel's job not to mix them up). The angel checks the impact on their health and asks each player to adjust their own health-o-meter, remembering two biscuits are needed to increase each player's health; one biscuit, health stays where it was; no biscuits and health drops.

*Monday Evening*

Next comes an opportunity for each survivor in turn to speak one or two lines as a commentary on the day. This commentary could be used to argue for a greater share for the next day – e.g. 'My health is now very low, so perhaps I should have an extra biscuit.' Encourage survivors to try to find a character's voice in these moments.

The angel chooses who speaks first, then it passes clockwise.

When all survivors have spoken, the angel speaks again:

*It's Monday evening, and the sun is setting.*

Here the angel should insert one or two notable incidents of the day, by way of recapping as a daily report: Did anyone die? Was anyone caught stealing?

Then:

*You all go to sleep, and close your eyes.*

*But perhaps you wake during the night, determined to take another biscuit.*

*Keep your eyes closed, but if you choose to wake up and try to take one more biscuit, then open one of your hands resting on the table. You may or may not be successful*

*If you choose not to do this, then keep your hands where they are.*

The angel then places one biscuit in the open hands of at most two survivors. It's up to them which thieving players they reward with a biscuit – a choice based on what they think may make for the most interesting consequences – and they may choose for none to receive a biscuit. Survivors may be stealing biscuits for themselves, to preserve their own health, or to give to others. (If they are playing a specific character, it's important their behaviour is in keeping with that.)

*Tuesday*

And then it's Tuesday morning, and everyone wakes up. And the angel reads their opening script again, but this time, of course, it's Tuesday morning…

And the gameplay follows as Monday: first biscuits, then discussion, then sleep (and possible theft).

On Tuesday morning – and every following morning – the group's angel should secretly and randomly set on which day the ship may arrive by rolling a dice at the start of each day:

if they throw a 6, the survivors will see smoke on the horizon today, meaning a rescue ship will arrive tomorrow.

Angels must never tell the group that the ship will arrive tomorrow, or reveal the dice; the angels may choose to make various signs and omens happen; for instance, a rainbow appearing over the ocean, which is, of course, open to interpretation.

*Wednesday*

As before.

If the ship didn't arrive today, the angel rolls a dice: if you get a 4, 5 or 6, the survivors see smoke, meaning the ship will arrive tomorrow.

*Thursday*

As before.

If the ship didn't arrive today, the angel rolls a dice: if you get a 3, 4, 5 or 6, they see smoke, meaning the ship will arrive tomorrow.

*Friday/The Final Day*

As before.

If the ship doesn't arrive today, it never will in time. So, this is the last day in play. Either roll a dice – or ask the angel to decide if the ship arrives today or not.

If the ship does not arrive, then the angel narrates a final evening ending, something along these lines:

*It's Friday evening, and the sun is setting.*

Here they might insert one or two notable incidents of the day, by way of recapping. Then:

*You all go to sleep, and close your eyes.*

*You still hope a ship will arrive in time, but alas, you are all doomed.*

*In a year's time, the wreckage of the raft will wash ashore on a beach in a faraway country.*

*What happened to those on board, a tragedy.*

*We mourn their lives.*

If the ship does arrive, then the angel narrates a final evening ending, something along these lines:

*It's Friday evening, and the sun is setting.*

Here they might insert one or two notable incidents of the day, by way of recapping. Then:

*But with the sound of a horn, a ship arrives in the nick of time.*

*Men with beards and in uniforms carry you on board.*

*The next day, you – the surviving children – are all set ashore, and you say goodbye to each other: you may never see each other again.*

*We celebrate their lives.*

**Angel Academy**
*Designed by Tassos Stevens,
with inspiration from playtesting by Melanie Frances
and Tassos Stevens*

*In Brief*

This is a game about storytelling as a sequence of beats of 'What happens next?', and how this question plays in an audience's mind whenever they watch a story. If you go to the loo during a film at the cinema, the first question you ask when you're back to your seat is 'What happened?'

It casts players as teams of trainee angels, learning how to make the most interesting stories in the lives of humans. Each team devises a sequence of beats to tell a story based on a scenario; the most interesting story perhaps winning a prize in a friendly contest between teams.

After playing this game, you can cast some of your group for *The Biscuit Game* in the role of angels intervening in the scenario of *Life Raft*, deciding the events that happen to the raft and the survivors to help make the most interesting story happen.

Many religions around the world hold an idea of angels or other beings who look over the lives of humans. This game is a playful framing of angels, rather than based on any specific faith, but hopefully open enough to resonate.

*Useful Practice and References*

A useful reference is the improv game *What Happens Next?* by Keith Johnstone, which itself is the question that every audience is asking at the crucial beats in a story.

It's useful for directors and theatre-makers to view storytelling as *making a story happen with an audience* – and with the audience's expectations and investment, rather than by the writer alone.

The best answer to the question of 'What happens next?' for an audience might be 'What I didn't realise I wanted to happen next' – the 'Aha! Of course!' moments.

For example, in the *Life Raft* text, the way Ann divides the boat into two halves on day three, embodying the psychological divide and dramatically raising the stakes (pages 99–101). Everything ratchets up from this point forward.

We can frame a story as being a sequence of crucial beats of 'What happens next?', each beat being *a moment of change* – something happens that changes things for the characters, and/or also in the audience's expectations of how they think *the big questions* of a narrative may be resolved in the end.

In *Life Raft*, the big questions are: will they be rescued, who will survive, and what will that take?

Part of keeping a story interesting is keeping these big questions unanswered and in play until the best possible moment.

A great piece of dramaturgical advice from the creators of *South Park* is a useful tip for crafting the next beat to keep a story interesting: the *not 'and then' but 'because' or 'but'* rule. If the next beat of a story starts with 'and then...' then you'll have a boring story; it's better for it to start either with 'but...' or 'therefore...'

*The Gameplay*

You (the leader/teacher) play the role of an *angel trainer*; the players are *trainee angels*.

Their goal is to make and judge the most interesting story to happen, and graduate as angels.

Each team makes a story from a sequence of beats, based on a scenario.

The stories are then shared and judged. You could award a prize to the best story to make this a friendly contest.

*Scenario*

Choose a human scenario in which the angels may intervene.

In the case of *Life Raft*, the scenario is: a lifeboat adrift in the open ocean, with thirteen children and a dwindling supply of food.

You could choose another scenario; for instance:

- A king with three daughters, making plans for his succession.
- A boy and a girl each from rival families are going to the same party.
- A bride runs away with the best man the night before her wedding.
- Two hitmen wait in a basement for their victim to arrive.
- A police inspector interrupts an engagement party with questions about a suicide.
- A family receives a large life-insurance payout after the death of their father.
- An advertising executive tries to rebrand himself by changing his identity.
- A group of friends discover a spooky old cinema in the basement of a manor house.
- A family occasion is interrupted by the arrival of a long-lost sister.
- A mute child turns up outside the tent of some friends camping out in a storm.

Feel free to invent your own, which don't have to be based on known plays. But each team has to start with the same scenario.

You can discuss ideas for what might be the big questions in the audience's mind for the scenario – e.g. Who will end up with the king's crown? Will the course of true love run smooth? Will the family accept the sister back? Can you ever escape yourself?

Each team chooses a big question they want to play in the scenario. It could be that every team plays the same big question or chooses a different one.

*Teams*

Divide the group into teams of three to five players, with at least three and at most seven teams. Each team should have sheets of paper and a marker pen.

In each team, one player is *the guardian (of the story) angel*. They don't suggest changes to happen, but discuss ideas and have a casting vote if needed. They want to make the most interesting story happen. They have the marker pen.

The rest of the team will suggest changes to happen in each beat. They are either *angels of good fortune* – who want to make a happy ending to the story, or a harmonious answer to the big question. Or *angels of bad fortune* – who want to make an unhappy ending to the story, or a tragic answer to the big question.

*Beats*

You can play either a three-beat or a five-beat game, depending on the time available. It's probably best to start with a three-beat game to grasp the basics of how to play.

The challenge for each team is to devise a sequence of three beats, one beat at a time, to make the most interesting storyline for their scenario.

Each beat is a change – either/both an external change, which is an event in the situation of the scenario – or/and an internal change, which is in the heart of one or more people in the situation.

For example, an earthquake strikes the city just as the party is about to finish, or the boy and the girl spot each other and fall in love (although he already has a girlfriend).

Beats can be big or small. Many angel academies regard as virtuosos the angels who can alter fate with the smallest event, the lightest touch.

*The First Beat*

The angels of good fortune and angels of bad fortune suggest one idea each for the first beat, towards a harmonious ending or a tragic ending. These are then discussed. The guardian angel cannot suggest ideas, but has the final say over which beat is chosen. They write the beat with the marker pen on their first sheet of paper, and lay it on the table.

The angel trainer – aka you – might want to ask a couple of teams to share their first beats in this punctuation. Judgement over what makes a good beat is entirely subjective, but will likely effect a change in the situation, and leave you wondering what happens next.

*Repeat* (*and Repeat*)

And then repeat this for the second beat.

And then finally, the third beat.

But don't share these, ready for judging.

*Some Examples*

Scenario: Three witches tell a nobleman it is his destiny to be king.
Beat one: He goes on a killing spree, including murdering the current king.
Beat two: The nobleman becomes king (but starts going mad).
Beat three: The dead king's son storms the palace and kills the nobleman in revenge.

Scenario: A boy and girl from rival families fall madly in love.
Beat one: He kills her cousin in a fight and has to flee.
Beat two: She fakes her own death (to get out of being married to someone else).
Beat three: She does it so well that he thinks it's real and kills himself too.

(Shakespeare's plots generally suit five beats better, but you get the idea.)

Scenario: A police inspector interrupts an engagement party with questions about a suicide.
Beat one: His questions reveal they were all connected to the victim in different ways.
Beat two: The engaged couple break up when it turns out he fathered a child with the victim.
Beat three: The police inspector turns out not to be real and everyone freaks out.

Scenario: An advertising executive tries to rebrand himself by changing his identity.
Beat one: He leaves his troubles behind and gets a whole new life.
Beat two: But the experience drives him mad, giving him visions of his own death.
Beat three: In trying to escape it, he brings it about.

Scenario: A group of friends discover a spooky old cinema in the basement of a manor house.
Beat one: They discover a projector that can screen their dreams.
Beat two: It also opens a door to the dreamworld and they become trapped in one.
Beat three: After one of them volunteers to stay, the rest return unharmed.

*Sharing and Judging*

Each team in turn has a short time (30–60 seconds) to share their three-beat stories, before judgement.

There are many ways you can judge the stories. The quickest way is for you (as angel trainer) to decide which one you judge the best; as a tip, listen to the reaction in the room when each story is pitched, for laughter or 'oohs' or applause, and award the prize to the story that draws the strongest reaction.

(There might be a tendency towards silliness the first time you play this game, to add outrageous events just for the reaction. Let them get it out of their system, then point out that in stories, silliness affects *credibility*. Audiences are willing to suspend disbelief, but only up to a point. Challenge the players to generate the same reaction with a story we actually believe.)

With more time, you could ask the teams to award points to other teams' stories. For instance, each team gets 5 points that they have to give to two stories by other teams – splitting either 4 and 1 points, or 3 and 2 points between whichever two stories they liked the most. Teams also give the reasons behind their judgement. The teacher can then award 5 points to the team who give the best-reasoned judgement.

If you are going on to play *The Biscuit Game*, you may want to finish *Angel Academy* by giving the scenario of a group of children stuck on a life raft with dwindling supplies of food. Keep a note of the ideas generated, as these could be used later, especially if you start adding random events with dice rolls (see page 157).

**A Life Well Played**
*Designed by Tassos Stevens*

*In Brief*

This is a short storytelling game for a player to reflect on the life of a character they have been playing in *The Biscuit Game* when they exit that game.

Before playing *The Biscuit Game*, the player decides on some basic biographical information, and writes answers to three questions about their character's values, personality and relationships.

With larger groups, you could have each character played by a pair: one performer and one director/coach. This is also a way of pairing participants into mutually beneficial partnerships, with only one of them taking part in the improvisation, and the other being the director of their actions between scenes. If so, then they answer questions together, with the director/coach having final say.

When everyone plays their character in *The Biscuit Game*, they do their best to live by any or all of their answers to the questions.

When they exit play, they have one minute in the spotlight to tell the story of their character's experience, in a police interview after the lifeboat is rescued.

After their one-minute interview, they then ask one of the questions they have chosen to play, and everyone else decides what they think the spotlit player's answer might be, based on how they played in the game. The spotlit player then reveals their answer.

## 152  LIFE RAFT

*Useful Practice and References*

- The confessional/diary room in reality TV shows, where players reflect and tell the story of what happened in play.
- Aristotle's *eudaimonia*, as the happiness in a life well lived, and the deathbed perspective on life.
- The director–actor collaboration.

*The Gameplay*

Players are gathered before playing *The Biscuit Game*. They each have a sheet of paper and pen.

Individually, they should give their character a name and an age and write it down.

Next, they choose three adjectives to describe their character's personality and state when they enter the boat.

In the *Life Raft* character list on page 13, after their name and age, each character is given three adjectives to describe their general traits, as follows:

ALLAN, *fourteen, thinker, impressionable, reluctant leader.*
ANN, *thirteen, cocky, confident, frightened.*
GEORGE, *twelve, caring, jealous, easily led.*
ALFIE, *thirteen, gruff, stubborn, physically strong.*
ARCHIE, *twelve, gentle, kind, terrified.*
ROGER, *thirteen, chivalrous, logical, sceptical.*
SAM, *twelve, laddy, gullible, daydreamer.*
MARGARET, *twelve, hysterical, competitive, afraid.*
MARGOT, *eleven, immature, obedient, religious.*
ENID, *thirteen, pugnacious, superior, judgemental.*
ANTHEA, *eleven, kind, innocent, practical.*
AMY, *eleven, introverted, traumatised, seriously injured.*

Feel free to choose from these, or also make up your own. If you are rehearsing and performing the full play, then everyone can play in character.

The most useful character qualities for a performance game are those you can actively play. Try not to have too many, as it's hard to play more than three.

Once everyone has decided on their three adjectives, introduce the characters to one another.

During these introductions, ask them to look for *rivalries* and *loyalties*. These happen along predictable lines:

- *Age* – especially where different ages are treated differently – e.g. the eldest may be more likely to be a leader.
- *Values* – e.g. are you someone who believes in competition, or someone who believes in cooperation?
- *Relationships* – is there another character here you're looking out to protect, or someone you hope will get washed overboard?

Finally, each survivor now needs to secretly write the answers to three questions about themselves.

The questions can be the same three for every player, or they could be presented with a shortlist of questions to choose three from. Here's a starter list:

- Which other character do they care about the most in this scenario? (This could be any relationship, family, friend, sweetheart, etc.)
- Which other character do they dislike the most in this scenario?
- If 10 is the most commanding in the room, and 1 is the least commanding, which number would match them?
- If 10 is someone who likes to be in the social spotlight, and 1 is someone who prefers to stay in the shadows, which number would match them?
- If the character's energy were a colour, which colour would it be?
- What are the character's moral priorities (e.g. selfishness versus altruism)?

You could also devise questions with the whole group beforehand.

Then play *The Biscuit Game* again, with everyone trying to stay true to their character.

At the end of the game, tell the group that the police want to interview each of them individually about their experience on the boat.

One by one, everyone takes the spotlight and tells the story of the game from their character's perspective for one minute. You could ask one of the guardian angels to double as the interviewing officer.

One rule: players are not allowed to refer explicitly to any of the questions they answered, or their answers.

As a tip, it's often easier to pick one or two specific key moments in play and talk about those, rather than more generally.

Time this, so that they each have precisely one minute. They don't have to speak for the whole time, they can be silent in parts, but they must occupy the spotlight for one minute.

They then ask *one* of the questions they answered before play. Everyone else decides what they think the spotlit player's answer might be, based on how they played and the story they told, before the player reveals their answer.

If either the angel or the majority of the room agree that the player's answer chimes with how they played and the story they told, then that player wins – and enters story heaven.

**Playing and Developing the Games**

It's recommended that you start by playing *The Game's Afoot* with your class or group, to open up the framework of game-making, and to distribute creative agency in the room. It's also a ready-made warm-up.

Then you might play the basic version of *The Biscuit Game* in two or three smaller groups, with one angel facilitating the gameplay for ten to fifteen players. This will give you all a feel for how it plays.

After that, you could do some character development with *A Life Well Played*, including each character's one-minute police-interview speech. This game is important for motivating players to make choices that are dramatically interesting, even if they end in an early death.

Then you might play *Angel Academy*, ending with the scenario of *Life Raft*, and use it to generate ideas for events – both big and small – that the angels can make happen when you next run *The Biscuit Game*.

You might also consider the suggested avenues for changing and enriching *The Biscuit Game* outlined in the 'Options for Game-changing' section below.

And then check in with your group, and together figure out how best for you to integrate the games into one playing experience. More notes about this follow.

*Playing Scale*

*The Biscuit Game* is the main engine of gameplay for your performance game.

It's up to you and the group to decide the *playing scale*: how many characters are on board the life raft. As a rule of thumb, more characters means more complexity – both richer and noisier. The original play has thirteen characters; often for this kind of group-play anywhere between eight and sixteen players might be an ideal scale.

If you have a larger group, you might assign two players as a pair to one character. One of the players will perform the character in the game; the other will direct or coach them. In a punctuation point of the gameplay – e.g. at the end of the night before the next day – the pairs have a few minutes to discuss tactics and decisions played, and plan for what happens next.

You could also have two or three boats, each running separately, with one or two angels looking over them. Imagine, if you like, a flotilla of small lifeboats adrift in the ocean.

*Integrating Events*

You can run *Angel Academy* with the scenario of *Life Raft*, in order to generate ideas for beats, which are events that could happen in the course of playing a larger-scale version of *The Biscuit Game*.

You can introduce these events to all the boats simultaneously, or each boat's angel can take individual responsibility for it.

If you have a larger group, with a contingent who are more interested in writing than performing, once you have played *Angel Academy* with them, you can enhance the number and role of angels as follows:

- Each boat gets a small team of angels in addition to all the survivors.
- At least one is an angel of good fortune, suggesting events to make a harmonious ending happen.
- At least one is an angel of bad fortune, suggesting events to make a tragic ending happen.
- And one is the guardian (of the story) angel with editorial decision-making to make the most interesting story happen.

No events should happen on Monday, the first day in the gameplay.

Only one event should happen on Tuesday, the second day in the gameplay.

After that, either one or two events can happen each day, at the discretion of the guardian (of the story) angel.

Events can be seeded from character, an *internal* spark suggested by the players – for example, one character makes the case to throw another overboard, or perhaps another volunteers instead. In this character-led approach, players must actively play their adjectives.

Events can also come from an *external* spark – for example, a storm breaks, and one player is washed overboard.

Events can be *randomly* generated by a single dice roll, with options set in advance – for example:

- Roll a *1* – and it's a hurricane, and someone is blown overboard (roll again to decide who)
- Roll a *2* – and a wave washes half the remaining biscuits overboard.
- Roll a *3* – and some flying fish land on the boat providing a meal for two people.
- Roll a *4* – and an extra stash of six biscuits is discovered by one player (roll again to decide who).
- Roll a *5* – and a bottle floats past; its contents may be nutritious or poisonous (roll again to decide which).
- Roll a *6* – and… we'll leave you to come up with your own!

Try not to repeat an event, unless the repetition is interesting.

Events and their impact may be implacable, but there also may be a chance for a player to *intervene*. You can roll a dice to decide – e.g. a player can save another from being washed overboard if they roll a 4, 5 or 6.

Or you can use a *skills-test*: a simple, speedy challenge like *Rock Paper Scissors*, or repeat a tongue-twister. It's excellent if you can find a skills-test analogous to the real event – e.g. a player can save another from being washed overboard if they are able to throw a paper ball into a waste bin.

Might there be an additional consequence of failure? Like a near-miss actually means that player is washed overboard too?

Angels are invisible to other characters, so they can move freely within the scene, listening to conversations the better to come up with ideas for events, while not being able to go too close or touch characters.

Note that for a group of twenty-nine players (a whole school class, perhaps), you could cast thirteen characters each with a pair of players – one player, one coach – and also have three angels. You can adapt these best to suit the number of players.

## *Options for Game-changing*

It's recommended that you play a basic version of *The Biscuit Game* first of all to grasp the possibilities of the core gameplay. But as this may become a little repetitive, we'd recommend the group explores how best to develop it for richer performance, adding and changing elements and rules, as demonstrated in the game-changing process of *The Game's Afoot*.

Here are some suggestions you might like to explore, but we hope you and your group might come up with your own ideas... It's *your* game now!

SCENES

You can add a scene format for each day, which might play out before the daily decision on biscuit allocation. Rather than free improv, which might get messy, it's useful to have a more constrained format.

Here's a format for a *conversation scene*:

- There's a question that each player takes it in turn to answer, or chooses to pass.
- The question for conversation on the first day: Why should I survive?

For reference, look at pages 86–97 of *Life Raft* where the characters do this in turn.

Here's a format for an *interaction scene*:

- Everyone chooses one interaction they want to have in the scene – e.g. 'I want to convince someone to give me their biscuit.'
- One player starts their interaction with at least one other player.
- The next can either join that interaction, or start their own. Each player can only take part in one interaction per scene.

On page 58 of *Life Raft*, the stage directions at the start of day two give some examples of simple interactions between characters.

POWER AND DECISION-MAKING

How will the people on the life raft decide how to share the biscuits? You can set this, or you can let them decide their own decision-making process themselves. For instance, you might have the eldest – Allan and Ann in the play – deciding on a benevolent dictatorship, or at least having the casting vote. Or players might make proposals on a biscuit-sharing process, which is then voted on. One consequence of decision-making is…

PLAYING TIME

Putting it bluntly, democracy takes longer if there are more voices to be heard. In real life, it's worth it… but for the purposes of enjoyable gameplay, you should decide how to manage time. The angels may shout out if it's approaching noon, or sunset. Or they could set a time limit for a scene (wear a watch), and then have something happen to interrupt it (as a last resort, just blow a whistle).

And that's it!

We'd love to know how you get on.

You can reach us at fin@appliedstories.co.uk and theplayfuldoc@gmail.com.

**www.nickhernbooks.co.uk**

@nickhernbooks